THE PHILOSOPHY OF
PUDDINGS

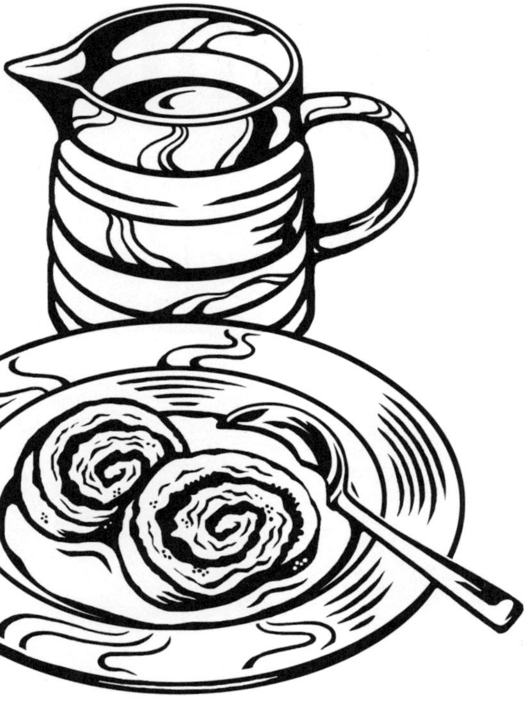

THE PHILOSOPHY OF
PUDDINGS

NEIL BUTTERY

BRITISH LIBRARY

First published 2024 by
The British Library
96 Euston Road
London NW1 2DB

Text copyright © Neil Buttery 2024
Illustrations from the British Library collections courtesy of the
British Library Board, and from other named copyright holders

ISBN 978 0 7123 5511 7
eISBN 978 0 7123 6843 8
Cataloguing in Publication Data
A catalogue record for this book is available
from the British Library

Designed and typeset by Sandra Friesen
Printed in China by C&C Offset Printing Co., Ltd.

CONTENTS

Introduction   1

The First Puddings   7

The Golden Age   19

Pudding and Identity   57

Pudding for Dessert   75

Twenty-First-Century Puddings   93

Further Reading and Selected References   99

List of Illustrations   101

Endnotes   105

- Apple and Pear Dumplings.
- Cold Apple Pudding.
- Apricot Fritters.
- Mince Pies.
- Galette.
- Apple Tart.
- Peach Tartlet.
- Pancakes and Apricot Jam.
- Coffee Custard à la Religieuse.
- Charlotte Russe.
- Apples and Rice.
- Cherry Tart.
- Apple Marmalade Tart.
- Olives.
- Roly Poly Jam Pudding.
- Meringues with Preserve.
- Apricot Tartlet.
- Christmas Plum Pudding.
- Charlotte of Pears.

INTRODUCTION

Blessed be he that invented pudding, for it is a manna that hits the palates of all sorts of people; a manna, better than that of the wilderness, because the people are never weary of it. Ah, what an excellent thing is an English pudding! To come in pudding-time, is as much as to say, to come in the most lucky moment in the world. Give an English man a pudding, and he shall think it a noble treat in any part of the world.

THE QUOTE ABOVE is by François Maximilien Misson, a French writer living in England in the 1690s. We can see by his wonderful writing just how surprised and amazed he was to discover this uniquely British foodstuff, a ragbag collection of preparations and an intrinsic element of both the nation's dinner table and its identity.

Misson also said that '[t]he pudding dish is very difficult to be described, because of the several sorts there are of it … They bake them in an oven, they boil them with meat, they make them fifty several ways.' For the British today, puddings conjure up a plethora of wonderful images that make us misty-eyed: jam roly-poly pudding and custard; Yorkshire pudding and onion gravy; the Burns Night haggis; sticky toffee pudding; flaming Christmas pudding. There are too, the perhaps less fondly remembered ones like black pudding and school sago pudding. But how can *all* of these very different foods be puddings? Then, if you add to the fact that pudding is also a byword for any sweet dessert, you see how confusing the term must be to non-Brits. It can't be done succinctly; the best Samuel Johnson could do in his dictionary of 1755 was: 'A kind of food very variously compounded but generally made of meal, milk and eggs.' It all seems eye-crossingly complicated until one traces the rich, long history of puddings, and sees their evolution as cooks across the British Isles adapted them to ever-changing tastes and technologies.

In *The Philosophy of Puddings*, I will lay out not just the story and history of the British pudding as a food, but its importance in our identity and language. Puddings are more than just a foodstuff. Key to their success, I believe, is that they are a truly democratic food, eaten by everyone, young and old, rich and poor. Today, pudding is one of the few great levellers.

You get an indication of how important pudding is to our identity by how it is used in language and metaphor. Samuel Johnson noted elsewhere in his diary that '[a] buffoon is called by every nation by the name of the dish they like best:

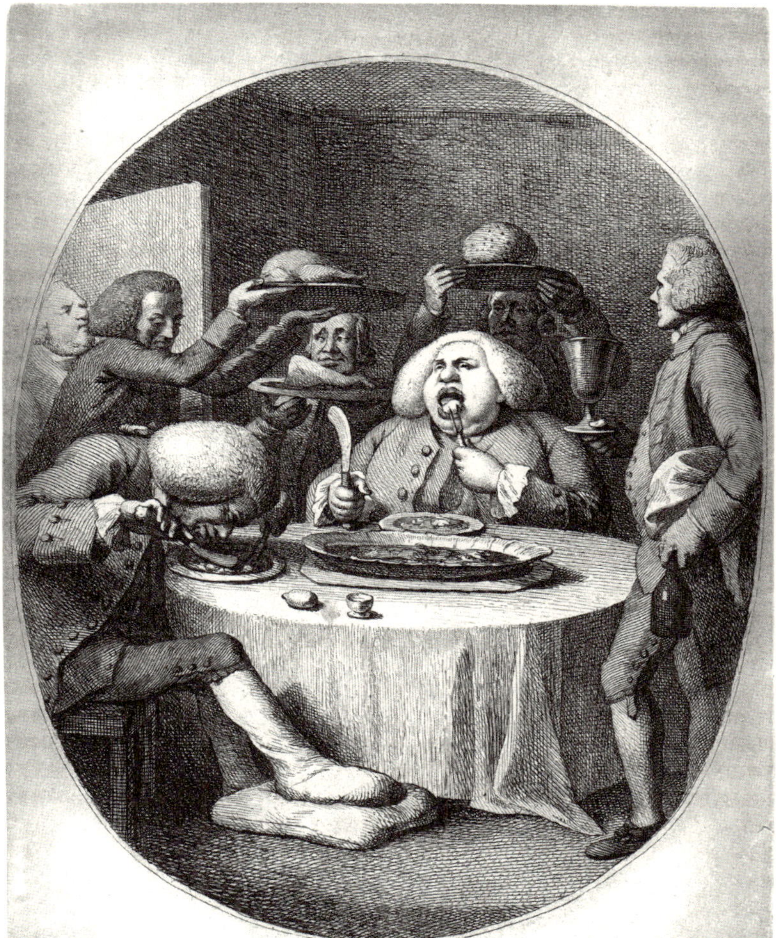

in French *jean pottage*, and in English *jack-pudding*.' The word pudding has also been used in the past as a slight for those who may have tucked away too much of it in their time; Hunter and Morris's *Universal Dictionary* (1897) has an entry, 'pudding-faced', used to describe a person who has 'a fat, round and smooth face like a pudding'. In *Henry IV Part I*, Prince Hal cruelly describes Falstaff as a 'roasted Manningtree ox with a pudding in its belly'.

There are several proverbs and sayings involving pudding: if you 'overegg the pudding', you have spoilt it by making it too rich. The best-known saying is 'the proof of the pudding is in the eating', meaning you shouldn't judge something by its appearance; instead wait until you have experienced it – puddings, especially boiled suet ones, don't always look pretty but, goodness, they are delicious. The saying is often misspoken as 'the proof is in the pudding', which rather misses the point.

I have been a lifelong pudding fan. As a child growing up in Yorkshire, some kind of pudding was provided after every meal: apple pie, rhubarb crumble, jam roly-poly, treacle sponge. As an adult enthusiasm was replaced by obsession when I decided to cook and blog every recipe in Jane Grigson's seminal classic *English Food* as a pet project to help me practise writing. That was almost 20 years ago; the blog was called *Neil Cooks Grigson*. Soon, one blog became two, the second being *British Food: A History*. Armed with my arsenal of traditional recipes, I started 'Pud Club', a pudding-only supper club where I could show off my favourite puddings to guests. The pop-ups became a bricks-and-mortar restaurant and there were always traditional puddings on the menu. Because I have blogged my progress, experiences and research for getting on two decades now, recipes for many of the puddings mentioned in this book appear within their virtual pages.

It's fair to say that I have cooked many puddings, and I have been taught by the greats, whose names may or may not be familiar: Eliza Acton, Thomas Dawson, Kenelm Digby, Robert May, Elizabeth Raffald, to name but a few. In this book, I have deliberately chosen primary sources that are well known and therefore easy to gain access to online. I hope that, once you have finished reading this book, you will seek out some of the texts.

The works of many other food historians and writers have been indispensable in researching this book: figures such as Peter Brears, Regula Ysewijn, Catherine Brown, Dorothy Hartley, Laura Mason, Ivan Day, Glyn Hughes and the aforementioned Jane Grigson. There is a list of key references for further reading at the back of this book.

But now let us begin our story, the great journey that the pudding has taken, and the many changes it has gone through. The word pudding, it is believed, comes from the French *boudin*, meaning sausage: the pudding's origins are visceral, a food made in guts. These are not humble beginnings though; the first puddings were food for the rich, for the high and mighty, the most *un*democratic of foods.

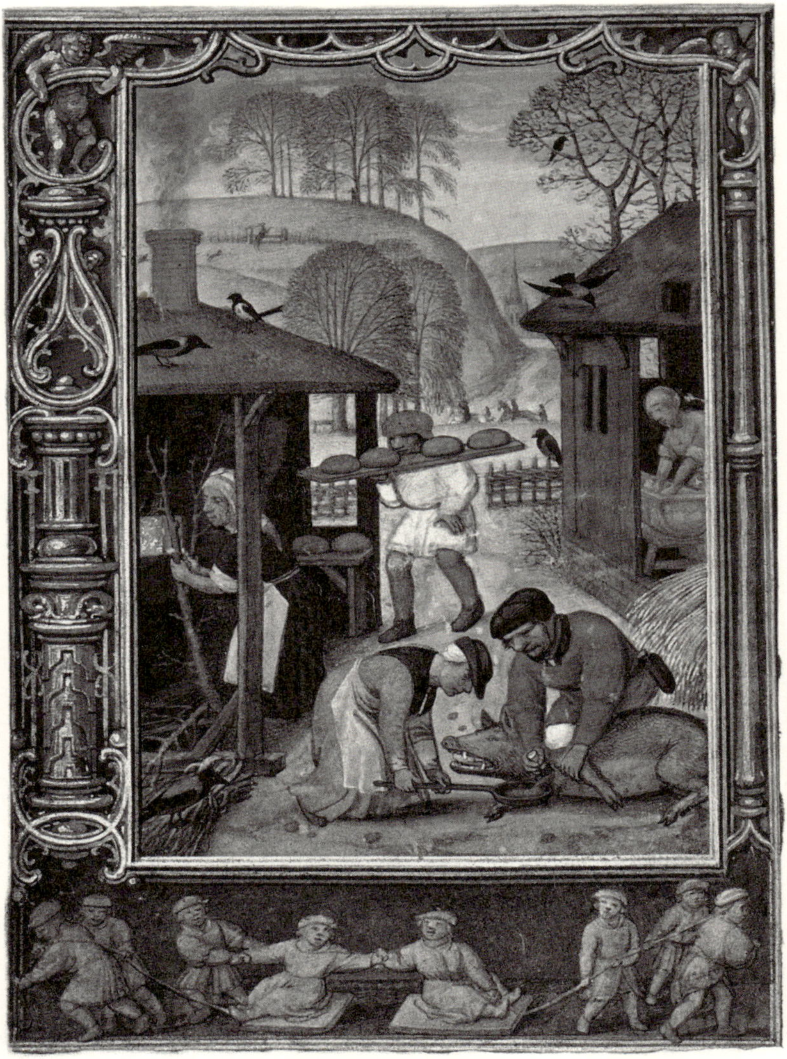

THE FIRST PUDDINGS

BLACK PUDDINGS ARE the first to be mentioned in English texts not just because they are delicious, but also because the acquisition of blood had to take place at the slaughter of an animal. Blood is a product of slaughter and it must be captured immediately or it is spoiled, washed away, a wasted resource. Dorothy Hartley described the process in *Lost Country Life* (1979): 'The house pig was usually slaughtered near the house ... and a capable woman attended to catch the blood as it spurted out after the pig had been "stuck".' Several medieval illuminated manuscripts show the killing of pigs and the immediate making of black puddings: it had to be so, wait too long and the blood will turn into clots. Black puddings require a length of intestine into which filling can be stuffed, which meant small households that kept one pig perhaps enjoyed black puddings once a year when the house pig was slaughtered. It was very different in the grand houses of the upper classes with their meat-rich diets; they ate puddings all the time.

Black puddings are the first to be described in ancient literature too: goats' stomachs filled with fat and blood are described in Homer's *Odyssey*; and in the *Satyricon*, written by Petronius in first-century Rome, pigs were served 'garlanded with sausages and ... blood-puddings and very nicely done giblets'. The first recipes, however, appear in the fifth-century Roman text *Apicius*. They are essentially a poached sausage – a mixture of minced or pounded meat or offal, blood, fat, cereals or breadcrumbs, and seasonings – stuffed into a section of animal gut, tied and boiled. One recipe, simply and unappetisingly called 'Stomach', is a pig's paunch stuffed with a mixture of ground pork meat, pig brains, pine nuts, eggs, fish sauce, oil and spices. It was boiled, smoked and served sliced with more fish sauce. These ingredients were the best ingredients money could buy, and status could allow.

The Romans are important to the story of the British pudding because, it seems, they were the ones who brought puddings and the art of pudding-making to the Britons: one dish described in *Apicius*, called *lucanica*, crops up centuries later in texts written in Old English. The ingredients are very similar and, most importantly, the name remained, suggesting that after the Romans exited England, their pudding and sausage-making skills were retained.

The first recipes in English are medieval and are for black pudding, and some of them are very similar to today's puddings: blood, suet and boiled oat groats are stuffed

PUDDINGS NOT IN GUTS

Before the pudding cloth caught on, puddings were sometimes made in things other than stomachs or guts, evidence perhaps that they have always wanted to burst out of their restraints. It also demonstrates how food and language adapt and interact over time. For example, in the seventeenth century you find recipes for whole animals used as the vessel for a pudding. In *The Good Housewife's Jewel* (1596), Thomas Dawson gives instructions 'To boil a carp in a green broth with a pudding in its belly', whereby the fish's cavity is filled with a mixture made from its roe, some bread, raisins and spices, then sewn up and simmered in broth. He also provides a recipe 'To make a pudding in a Breast of Veal'. Puddings have even been made in vegetables such as turnips and (large) carrots. A curious recipe crops up in a fifteenth-century manuscript for a 'poddyng of Capoun necke', where the offal of the bird is mixed with several typical pudding ingredients to make a nicely spiced stuffing mixture, and the neck skin is used to wrap it up before baking. We would call these 'stuffings' today, but it shows that pretty much any mixture of meat, fat and cereals bound and cooked inside something else was considered a pudding.

into guts, then boiled, cooled and fried. It's nice to see that some things have never changed. Modern black puddings are typically made with pig's blood, but the blood of other animals was used, including sheep and cattle. Hannah Glasse made a claim in 1747 that the Scots used the blood of geese in their black puddings, something later confirmed by Scots food anthropologist F. Marian McNeill, who wrote in *The Scots Kitchen* (1968) that they were eaten in rural areas well into the twentieth century. According to McNeill, the Scots liked to bleed their cattle so that they could make a pudding without killing any of their animals. Black puddings were even enjoyed during Lent, when the flesh of animals could not be eaten, and that included the gut casings too. Fish was allowed, and alternatives were devised such as pike pudding, a mixture of the flesh and liver of the creature, currants and saffron, all stuffed into its stomach, then simmered and served forth. One fifteenth-century manuscript has an astonishing Lenten recipe for a 'Puddung of purpaysse', porpoise black pudding. The blood and fat of 'hym' are combined with oatmeal, salt, black pepper and ginger, mixed 'to-gederys wel' and then stuffed into 'the Gutte of the purpays'. Even on fast days, the upper classes ate luxuriantly.

Puddings were so dearly loved, and so many animals were regularly slaughtered for food in the grand houses and monasteries of the Middle Ages, that women called 'pudding wives' were employed especially for the purpose of making puddings – Henry VIII employed one at Hampton Court. They were the only women allowed into the male-dominated kitchens of upper-class homes and monasteries. It was a job not in the least bit glamorous, her main tasks being the preparation of the meat and offal, then cleaning the entrails by rinsing and washing them several times. The fillings, once made and seasoned, were stuffed into a length of intestine already tied at one end. After filling, the other end was tied and then both ends were made doubly secure with small pegs called pudding pricks. It was important not to overfill one's guts because the contents tended to swell in cooking. An eagle eye was kept over the cooking puddings, needle at the ready to prick any air bubbles that formed, lest they cause the puddings to explode. It was a huge amount of smelly work.

The Tudor and Stuart eras were the golden period for puddings made in guts, and recipes for them abound in books by such writers as Hannah Woolley, Sir Kenelm Digby, Robert May and Gervase Markham. Black pudding was still very popular, but now there were white puddings, which today are generally made from pork fat, ground pork, rusk and white pepper – a fairly simple affair, but in the Early Modern period, any ingredients that were very pale in colour were fair game, and the recipes were opulent. In *The Closet of the Eminently Learned Sir Kenelme Digbie Knight Opened* (1669), one white pudding is made from a fillet of veal, 'a good fleshy capon', bacon, suet, twenty egg

Ætatis Suæ 71
1660

What wouldst thou view but in one face
all hospitalitie, the race
of those that for the Gusto stand,
whose tables a whole Ark comand
of Natures plentie, wouldst thou see
this sight, peruse Mays booke, tis hee.

THE
Accomplisht Cook
OR THE
ART & MYSTERY
OF
COOKERY.

Wherein the whole ART is revealed in a more easie and perfect Method, than hath been publisht in any language.

Expert and ready Ways for the Dressing of all Sorts of FLESH, FOWL, and FISH, with variety of SAUCES proper for each of them; and how to raise all manner of *Pastes*; the best Directions for all sorts of *Kickshaws*, also the *Terms* of CARVING and SEWING.

An exact account of all *Dishes* for all *Seasons* of the Year, with other *A-la-mode Curiosities*

The Fifth Edition, with large Additions throughout the whole work: besides two hundred Figures of several Forms for all manner of bak'd Meats, (either Flesh, or Fish) as, Pyes Tarts, Custards, Cheesecakes, and Florentines, placed in Tables, and directed to the Pages they appertain to.

Approved by the fifty five Years Experience and Industry of *ROBERT MAY*, in his Attendance on several Persons of great Honour.

London, Printed for *Obadiah Blagrave* at the *Bear and Star* in St. *Pauls Church-Yard*, 1685.

yolks, milk and cream, and a range of sweet spices. From the sixteenth century there are recipes for hog's puddings, which are considered a regional speciality of southwest England today but were once eaten enthusiastically all around the country. They differ from white puddings in that the meat came exclusively from pigs. In *The Good Housewife's Jewel* by Thomas Dawson, there's a delectable-sounding hog's pudding made of pig liver, cream, eggs and egg yolks, suet, raisins, cloves, mace, pepper, salt, sugar and grated bread.

In this period sugar and dried or candied fruits become steadily cheaper (though well out of the reach of the working and middle classes), so they feature much more compared to the Middle Ages, but there is no separation between what we think of today as sweet and savoury ingredients, explaining the existence of recipes that we would struggle to classify today. For example, Robert May in *The Accomplisht Cook* (1685) has a recipe for marrow pudding, a mixture of bone marrow, raisins, dates, sack (a sherry-like drink), rosewater, ambergris and musk. Some were very rich indeed: Elizabeth Cromwell – wife of Lord Protector Oliver Cromwell – breakfasted on a pudding made of equal weights of ground almonds, breadcrumbs and sugar, enriched with bone marrow and seasoned with nutmeg and ambergris, and it sounds most pleasant, but many recipes are not for the faint-hearted; the people of the Early Modern period were very partial, gung-ho even, with respect to offal. Robert May gives instructions 'To Make Puddings of a Heifers Udder'; in Hannah Glasse's *The Art of Cookery Made Plain and Easy* (1747) there is a pudding made with spinal cord; and Sir Kenelm Digby has a recipe for 'an Excellent Pudding', in which he instructs us to 'Take of the Tripes of Veal the whitest and finest you can find; wash them well. And let them lie in fair Fountain or River Water, till they do not smell like Tripes.' Good advice, I'd say.

At the beginning of the seventeenth century, an important change occurs: John Murrell provides a recipe for a 'Cambridge pudding', a type of bread pudding, in *A New Booke of Cookerie* (1615), and it is notable because it is the first in a whole slew of recipes where puddings are cooked not in guts, but in cloths. This may not seem significant, but the widespread adoption changed everything, setting the pudding on a divergent path from its kin, the sausages, to become something quite different. Puddings could be made much more frequently now that one didn't have to wait for an animal to be slaughtered to make one. Not only that but the cloth it was cooked in could be reused. Because puddings no longer required the death of an animal, their meat content reduced substantially, and if meat was to be served, it was cooked as a joint alongside the pudding in a pot or cauldron, or was roasted before the fire. As a consequence, savoury puddings became lighter and sweeter. As rich folk moved on to a different sort of pudding, the lower classes carried on eating the types of

HAGGIS

Haggis may be Scotland's national dish now but there is, in fact, nothing particularly Scottish about it. F. Marian McNeill described it as 'simply a super-sausage, and like the sausage, it was once common to many lands'. Today haggises are made from a sheep's pluck – the heart, liver, lungs and spleen – suet, pinhead oatmeal, onions, salt and lots of black pepper. 'Wash the pluck well and put on the boil covered with cold water,' wrote McNeill, 'letting the windpipe hang over the side of the pot to let out any impurities.' Then it is chopped and cooked again with the remaining ingredients until tender, stuffed into the sheep's stomach and boiled once more. Delicious as it may be in its traditional form, there used to be a great variety of different Scottish haggises. One, called 'Haggis Royal', was made with mutton, beef marrow, oats, anchovies, lemon zest, parsley, eggs and red wine, and sounds rather tasty.

All haggis recipes written before the eighteenth century are English. There was no fixed recipe and the term referred to any sort of pudding cooked in a stomach. The majority of recipes are rich and aromatic: take Thomas Dawson's 'Haggis Pudding' of calf's 'chauldron' (chitterlings), bread, suet, egg yolks, cream, rosewater, pepper, mace, 'nutmegs', herbs such as pennyroyal and thyme, and 'a good deal of sugar'. 'Why everyone except the Scots', wrote McNeill, 'stopped stuffing the paunch whilst they went on stuffing the intestines, the annals of gastronomy do not reveal.'

puddings made with guts – the puddings that in previous centuries they had been largely excluded from eating.

With the mass production and processing of food, and the suspicion associated with it, from the late-nineteenth century onwards, puddings made in guts fell out of favour. And in the twentieth century the days of making traditional black puddings were numbered too, after it was found that pigs urinate on slaughter, potentially contaminating the blood, and it became the norm to use dried blood instead. However, in the 1990s, black pudding had a resurgence in popularity when chefs started to use it as an ingredient, pairing it with scallops in particular. Since then, sales have continued to increase steadily, and the other puddings made in guts – white and hog's – have followed in black pudding's wake. There is even a (small-scale) commercial enterprise of fresh-blood black-pudding making. That we are exploring traditional methods once more is most exciting and encouraging, and long may it continue.

THE GOLDEN AGE

From the end of the seventeenth century, the pudding marches to the epicentre of Britain's food identity. Consequently, the number of pudding recipes in cookery books grew greatly. Going into the early Georgian era, an interesting new development occurred – puddings were being made in rather expensive china bowls. The glazed porcelain produced clean, neat lines, and made puddings that were easy to turn out. Always with an eye on food trends, the English potteries began to produce their own porcelain pudding moulds from around the 1860s. Though cheaper than imported china, English porcelain was still only affordable to the wealthy.

Aside from a bit of suet or bone marrow, meats were ditched and there was a single focus on the addition of exotic dried and candied fruits and sugar, plumped out with flour or breadcrumbs and bound with egg. But despite an increase in sweetness, there was still no clear distinction between sweet and savoury foods; sugar, after all, was a spice and used to season all sorts of foods. Dinner was served *à la française*, which means that several dishes were laid out on the dining table at the same time in two or three courses, and you chose what you fancied. For example, in *The Experienced English Housekeeper* (1769) by Elizabeth Raffald, there are settings for a 'Grand Table', and the second course is made up of pistachio cream, burnt cream (or, if you must, *crème brûlée*) and jellies, alongside roast hare, snipes in aspic, stewed cardoons (artichoke thistle) and mince pies. Very sweet confectionery, exotic fruits and ices were saved for the dessert course.

Female cookery writers of the eighteenth century, like Elizabeth Raffald, Hannah Glasse and Eliza Smith, were the real champions of the tradition of the plain and simple cookery for which the English used to be famous. They felt England had lost its way culinarily by focusing on lavish French cookery, which they thought wasteful and overly complex. Their books became best-sellers and their approach to cookery established what we think of today as traditional British food. Cookery books, once the trappings of the rich, were more affordable to the middle classes at a time when this cohort of society grew; more people were becoming better off thanks to the growing British Empire.

It was in the latter half of the eighteenth century that baked puddings became more common, as a technology cropped up that would make puddings even more versatile and available to even more people: the first cast-iron range ovens. Like most new technologies, they were very

2ᵈ Course

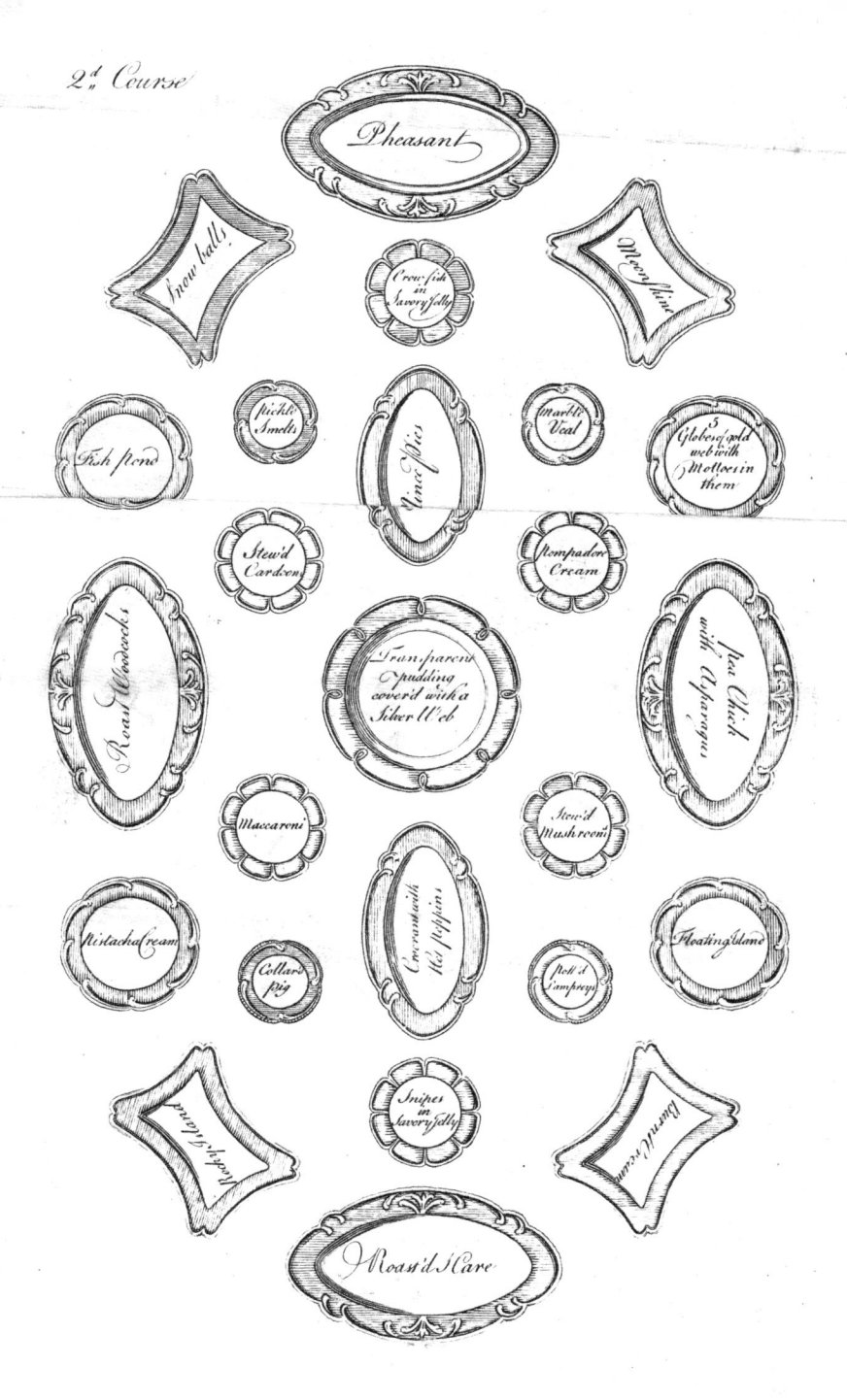

- Pheasant
- Snow balls
- Moonshine
- Crowfish in Savory Jelly
- Fish pond
- Pickle Smelts
- Lime Pies
- Marble Veal
- 3 Globes of gold web with Mottoes in them
- Stew'd Cardoon
- Pompadore Cream
- Roast Woodcocks
- Transparent Pudding cover'd with a Silver Web
- Pea Chick with Asparagus
- Maccaroni
- Stew'd Mushroom
- Pistacha Cream
- Crocant with Red pippins
- Roll'd Lamprey
- Floating Island
- Collar'd pig
- Rocky Island
- Burnt Cream
- Snipes in Savory Jelly
- Roast'd Hare

THE GOLD MEDAL
EAGLE RANGE.

Made in all Sizes from 2 ft. to 10 ft. wide.

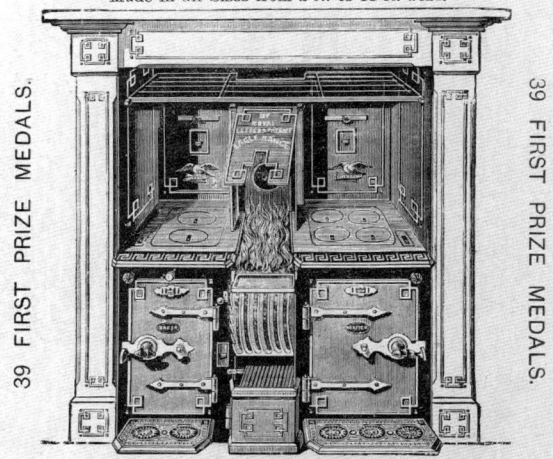

39 FIRST PRIZE MEDALS. **39 FIRST PRIZE MEDALS.**

SPECIAL ADVANTAGES.

1st.—This Range is independent of brick-setting. The flues are iron, very thick, and imperishable. Errors in setting, and consequent failure or erratic results, do not occur.

2nd.—The fire has an adjustable bottom grating, which, when raised in its highest position, will heat the ovens, hot-plate, and boiler perfectly; but, if a joint has to be roasted in front, the grating can be instantly lowered, and raised again when the roasting is done. This grating effects a great saving in fuel, never gets out of order, and gives results of the highest efficiency.

3rd.—The fire can be used open (as illustrated) or closed. The latter is for general cooking purposes, but, when cooking is not needed, the fire is opened. The opening of the fire reduces the draught, checks combustion, so that little attention is needed and little fuel used. It is cheerful for those in the kitchen, and grilling can be done on top if desired.

4th.—The pastry oven is fitted with a reversing damper, by which the heat can be directed to the top or the bottom, or equally; with this damper, puff pastry and other delicate things can be baked as efficiently as in a pastry-cook's oven. This is considered a great advantage by chefs, cooks, &c.

5th.—The ovens are perfectly ventilated, the inflowing air being warmed. There is no likelihood of the Range smoking, and its use is easily understood.

THE EAGLE RANGE AND FOUNDRY COMPANY,
176 REGENT STREET, & 58 ST. PAUL'S CHURCHYARD, LONDON.

CATALOGUES FREE.

expensive at first, but it meant that, for the first time, smaller homes could bake food in smaller batches and with more control. Stoves had stove tops, making boiling easier too. Now that your pudding could be boiled or baked, there began a further proliferation of puddings.

In the nineteenth century the Industrial Revolution made the production of moulds much cheaper, with the efficient stamping of tinned iron or copper sheets into hundreds of different designs. Cheaper moulds meant more folk could afford to buy them, and the number of recipes increased again. Not that the pudding cloth was left behind: plum puddings, for example, were still made this way. Eliza Acton has two chapters of pudding recipes, one of boiled, the other of baked, in *Modern Cookery for Private Families* (1845). Mrs Beeton assumed that the reader of her *Book of Household Management* (1861) had access to all the mod cons, because her huge puddings section is organised in alphabetical order, not by cooking method. In the second half of the nineteenth century, cookery books focused entirely on puddings were published, such as *Everybody's Pudding Book* (1862) by Georgiana Hill, and *Massey and Son's Comprehensive Pudding Book*, also in the 1860s, which contained over a thousand pudding recipes. By the close of the nineteenth century, even cheaper tinplate moulds were in production, so a pudding made in a nice mould was achievable in homes where there was someone there to prepare and cook one. In industrial towns and cities, this was a relative rarity, although families did get to enjoy a boiled pudding for Sunday dinner. But for those households where the housewife did stay at home, perhaps with some staff to aid her, puddings were served at every evening meal or lunchtime. Home economy received another boost at this time, when steamers were sold, which could cook puddings more quickly than boiling, giving them a lighter texture. When combined with a raising agent, puddings were positively fluffy. Roly-poly puddings, once boiled in a shirtsleeve in a short-pastry dough and therefore given the name of 'dead man's arm', were quite the stodge-fest, but when they were steamed, and the suet pastry included a touch of baking powder, they were transformed, creating something quite sublime.

It was at this time too that a change occurred to the nomenclature of puddings. It had been typical for cookery manuscripts to include recipes for puddings with legends like 'a good pudding', 'an excellent pudding' or 'another excellent pudding', but in the Victorian era there were scores of cookery books and literally hundreds of different puddings. Now puddings were demarked by region: dripping pudding became Yorkshire pudding; a standard suet and date pudding was suddenly from Cambridge; there was Bakewell pudding and Manchester pudding – place names helping them to stand out from the others. Sometimes they were named after certain demographics (poor man's pudding was basic, bachelor's pudding was small and easy

SPECIMENS FROM
THE BOOK OF MOULDS,
Containing 68 pages of Illustrations, published by
MARSHALL'S SCHOOL OF COOKERY
And sent Post Free on application.

TIN MOULDS.

No. 72A.
5¼ in., 5s.

No. 72B.
5¼ in., 5s.

No. 72C.
5½ in., 4s. 9d.

No. 72D.
5¼ in., 5s.

No. 72E.
5¼ in., 5s.

No. 72F.
5¼ in., 5s.

No. 73.
5½ in., 3s. 9d.

No. 74.
5½ in., 4s.

No. 75.
5½ in., 5s. 6d.

No. 76.
5¼ in., 3s. 9d.

No. 77.
5½ in., 4s.

No. 78.
6 in., 4s. 9d.

Advertisements. 1

COWAN'S BAKING POWDER

IS RECOMMENDED BY

MRS. A. B. MARSHALL.

READ HER TESTIMONIAL BELOW.

This Registered Label (but with pink cross lines) is on every Tin.

> **THE BEST QUALITY**
> **Cowan's Baking Powder**
> NONE GENUINE UNLESS SIGNED
> *C. C. Cowan*
> MADE WITH
> **Ingredients of the Finest Quality only.**
>
> Important Testimonial from Marshall's School of Cookery.
>
> *I find Cowan's Baking Powder is most excellent and I shall always use it and recommend it in preference to others.*
>
> 30, MORTIMER ST., W.   *Agnes B. Marshall*
>
> **COWAN & CO.,**
> Union Place, Wells Street, London, W.

Small, Medium, or Large Tins (nominal, 6d., 1s., and 2s. 6d.)
sold at the usual cash prices by Stores, Grocers, &c.
4½d., 9d., and 1s. 10d.

to make), ranks (diplomat pudding, chancellor's pudding) or monarchs and their consorts. Eliza Acton provides a recipe called Her Majesty's Pudding, which is a boiled custard pudding served with a fruit compote. She even goes as far as including a Saxe-Gotha Pudding. What pudding could be worthy enough to be named after a whole royal house? Why, a baked soufflé pudding, of course! Very cutting-edge for the home cook at this time. Mrs Beeton has an Empress Pudding, which is a rice pudding baked in a pastry case spread with jam. I can't help but feel she could have tried a little harder with that one.

AN INORDINATE FONDNESS FOR PUDDINGS

Let us now take a look at the main types of puddings enjoyed by the British in the eighteenth and nineteenth centuries and beyond.

Suet Puddings and Dumplings

If puddings were a taxonomic kingdom, suet puds would be a phylum, for it is a large and varied group. A suet pudding could be something as simple as a mixture of suet, water and flour or breadcrumbs steamed atop a simmering stew. A couple of rungs up the ladder, there is the spotted dick, boiled or steamed and made with milk instead of water, plus currants, a little sugar, self-raising flour, and a little lemon

PEASE PUDDING

As soon as the pudding cloth caught on, pottages – thick soups – were adapted to being cooked in a cloth and therefore deemed puddings. The best known of these is pease pudding. The working classes ate a lot of it, as the famous rhyme used in the children's hand-clapping games asserts:

> Pease-pudding hot,
> Pease-pudding cold,
> Pease-pudding in the pot,
> Nine days old.
>
> Some like it hot,
> Some like it cold,
> Some like it in the pot,
> Nine days old.

There was a decline in popularity in the eighteenth century, when peas were ditched for the new wonder-vegetable, the potato. It continued to be popular in northwest England, where peas grew much better than many other staple crops.

Pease pudding is very simple to prepare. In its most basic form, soaked split peas are loosely tied in a cloth and hung in simmering water, tethered to the pot handle with a length of twine. When the contents are soft and swollen, they are removed and seasoned with pepper, mint and a little sugar, mashed and mixed with an egg or two, re-tied and simmered again. This all seems rather more complicated than just making a simple pottage, so why adapt it into a pudding? First, it meant other things could be cooked in the pot at the same time, but more importantly, cooking the peas in a cloth meant that they didn't stick and burn on the base of the saucepan as they are prone to do, allowing the cook to essentially forget about it and concentrate on other things. Dorothy Hartley wrote in *Food in England* (1954): 'if well made the pease should have swollen together so that it comes out like a large, green cannonball', hot and steaming before being promptly opened up with two forks (never cut) and crowned with a large knob of butter or bacon fat.

Macédoine of Fruits.

Jelly with whipped Cream.

Pine Apple

Charlotte of Pommes.

Strawberries.

Mixed Fruits.

Apricots.

Chantilly Basket.

Christ

Custards.

Chocolate Cake.

Rice Croquettes.

Tartlets.

Red and white Currants.

Wedding Cake.

Compote of Pears.

Neapolitan Cake.

Pl. IV.

and Grapes.

Cherries.

Ice Pudding.

Lemon Jelly.

Melon and Green figs.

Candied Oranges.

Plums.

Ribbon Jelly.

Pudding.

Ices.

Meringues.

Sponge Cake.

Greengages.

Open Tart.

Plum Cake.

Compote of Apples.

Gâteau.

zest should there be any to hand. Plum duff, Christmas pudding and clootie dumpling sit on the enriched end of the suet-dumpling scale. Roly-polies, being a rolled-up piece of suet pastry, fit into this category. There are savoury ones, and bacon was popular, but it's the sweet ones – jam, lemon curd, treacle, mincemeat – that we all remember fondly. Dorothy Hartley described the roly-poly as 'a solid English pudding'; only in the pudding world could the word 'solid' be taken as a positive. Suet pastry can be used to line a basin and filled with steak, kidney and – if lucky – a few oysters. These are the only style of meaty puddings still extant, but if you think about it, a meat suet pudding is merely an inverted stew and dumplings, with the dumplings on the outside and stew in the middle. There are many sweet ones too, of course, such as apple hat, which is essentially an apple pie in pudding form. Other pastry doughs have been used in the past, but suet won out in the realm of the boiled and steamed pudding; it holds together better than other pastries and it can absorb juices without becoming overly stodgy.

One infamous suet pud in this style is Sussex pond pudding. It is quite the thing to behold: a pudding basin is lined with suet pastry, a whole lemon (stabbed a few times so that it will eventually split and let out its juices) is sat inside, and any space is filled with a mixture of whipped butter and brown sugar. It's covered with more pastry, sealed and steamed for at least four hours. When turned out onto a dish, it promptly collapses, creating a moat of sweet, lemony butter, the fruit within as soft as curd. Its origins are seventeenth century, but it was rather different then; the buttery insides are there, but tart apple is used instead of sour lemon. In one nineteenth-century recipe, the filling is just butter and sugar. The first time a whole lemon was used in a pudding, at least in a printed recipe, was in the 1970s, in Jane Grigson's *English Food*. From where this addition came, no one seems to know.

Bread Puddings

Almost every pudding is given some kind of integrity by some kind of starchy food. There's good old wheat flour, of course, or oatmeal, semolina, arrowroot and even potato. However, possibly the best, and certainly the most interesting, farinaceous foodstuff is bread. Bread puddings are perfect for the shrewd home economist because stale bread can be elevated, transformed even, with just a few basic store-cupboard ingredients into a whole range of superlative puddings.

In every stage of pudding evolution, bread puddings make an appearance, and the first detailed recipe for a bread pudding cooked in guts appears in Gervase Markham's *The English Huswife* (1615). It contains lots of eggs, a spice mix of cloves, mace, nutmeg, sugar, cinnamon, saffron and salt, two loaves of bread, grated, 'a great store of currants' and 'sheep's, hog's, or beef suet cut small'. The guts are

DEATH BY BREAD PUDDING

Making delicious sticks-to-your-ribs puddings from leftover bread makes for excellent home economics, but the ingredients must still be of excellent quality. Unfortunately, there was one incident where the ingredients certainly were not – and it led to the death of two people, including a child. According to a report written in an 1878 edition of *The Pharmaceutical Journal* by Dr Alfred H. Allen of the Sheffield School of Medicine, it is a sorry tale indeed. The incident occurred in a café and bakery in Barnsley, owned by a Mr Thresh, who had been accumulating scraps of leftover bread for a bread pudding. Nothing wrong with that, of course, except that he had been sequestering them for a full week, and some of the bread had been picked from half-eaten ham sandwiches. All who ate his pudding fell violently ill, and a waiter and Thresh's own three-year-old son died. Dr Allen found that the bread was very mouldy and concluded that the mould was the notorious ergot fungus; symptoms of ergot poisoning include

> vomiting, seizures, mania and psychosis. We don't know what happened to Mr Thresh or his café-bakery. That the sorry incident happened is, of course, tragic, but it is one of many, I am sure, which fuel the argument that puddings and other foods made from leftovers are inferior, which they definitely are not. Shockingly, one-third of all bread baked in the United Kingdom is thrown away. A travesty. Just think of the scores – thousands – of wonderful, satisfying puddings that were never cooked: if you make just one pudding after reading this book, please let it be a bread pudding!

filled, boiled and then 'cooked', one presumes fried, like a white pudding. One hundred and fifty years on, Elizabeth Raffald's recipe is almost identical, except it is boiled in a cloth.

Then we have the puddings made with sliced bread, the best being bread and butter pudding. Any sort of bread will work here: brioche, panettone, hot cross buns, teacakes… Of course, the bread must be lavishly buttered with real butter. Some like to add apricot jam, but I think that this is a pudding that eats better if made without too much sugar. Don't go fussy on the custard either. It should be a whole-egg custard made with a mixture of cream and milk; just make sure there is plenty – it's astounding how much is soaked into the bread in the baking. Rather more upmarket is summer pudding: a pudding basin lined with white bread and filled with lightly-cooked summer fruits. It first appeared at the turn of the twentieth century, with the curious name of 'hydropathic pudding', and it was made specifically for ladies staying in health spas, who desired a lower-calorie alternative to heavy suet puddings.

Bread pudding (not to be confused with bread and butter pudding) is a baked pudding particular to southeast England, but was once eaten all over the country. It's made by tearing up stale bread and soaking it in water (or tea). The bread is squeezed to remove excess liquid, then mixed with suet, cloves, cinnamon, allspice, dried fruit, sugar and eggs. The earliest example of a 'wrung-out' style of bread pudding I could find is in Elizabeth Hammond's *Modern Domestic Cookery, and Useful Receipt Book* of 1816. I suspect the dish is centuries older, but because the recipe is basic and made by working-class (rather than upper-class) families, the recipe wasn't captured in their books.

For some, having to eat anything involving soggy bread is a stomach-churning prospect, but there are some bread-based puddings that are nice and crisp: a Charlotte is made by lining a very well-buttered soufflé dish with fingers of stale bread, spooning in a filling of cooked apple, covered with more bread, then brushing that with more butter and baking it. Turned out, it makes a handsome dish, with beautifully golden, buttery, crisp bread. It was poshed up rather as a Charlotte Russe in the Regency era by Antonin Carême, which involved boudoir biscuits (ladyfingers), jelly and bavarois. *Not* a Charlotte in my opinion, just a neatly arranged trifle.

Sponge Puddings

For many, a steamed sponge pudding is the epitome of the steamed and boiled puds: treacle, lemon, jam and ginger are the classics, but there are others, like the black cap with its zingy blackcurrant topping. You can let your imagination run riot with flavours, fruits, spices and confections. Sponge puddings rely on a chemical leavening, but the first examples pre-date the widespread use of baking powder. The first I can find is Eliza Acton's Prince Albert

Pudding, which is made light with the addition of whisked eggs and sugar, rather like a Savoy or genoise cake batter. Sponge puddings were easily modified for oven baking, my personal favourites being Eve's pudding (stewed apples covered in a sponge cake mixture), pineapple upside-down cake and, of course, sticky toffee pudding.

Batter Puddings

The only batter pudding we cook up regularly is Yorkshire pudding, but there used to be a great variety, both sweet and savoury. They have their origins in boiled puddings and, I must admit, a boiled Yorkshire pudding doesn't seem very inviting: what makes a baked batter pudding so sublime is the texture contrast between crispy outsides and soft interior, but a pudding that's just soft batter does sound off-putting. A variation on a plain Yorkshire pudding is, of course, toad-in-the-hole, where sausages are baked into the batter. Some boiled batter puddings contained meat too, but I don't think they would go down very well today, well not if Elizabeth Raffald's 1769 recipe for sparrow dumplings is anything to go by:

> Mix half a Pint of good Milk, with three Eggs, a little Salt, and as much Flour as will make it a thick Batter, put a Lump of Butter rolled in Pepper and Salt in every Sparrow, mix them in the Batter, and tie them in a Cloth, boil them one Hour and a Half, pour melted Butter over them, and serve it up.

Small birds notwithstanding, batter puddings sound much better when they have something else added to them: sweet Kentish cherry batter pudding, which is baked or fried these days, was once boiled in a cloth.

Yorkshire Pudding

Combined with roast beef, the Yorkshire pudding is one of our most treasured national dishes. So integral is it to our collective food consciousness, it feels like it has been with us forever. The first time a recipe for one appears in print is within the pages of Hannah Glasse's *The Art of Cookery Made Plain and Easy* (1747), where she calls it 'an exceedingly good pudding'. But the recipe is not Glasse's; she adapted it from a cookery book published just a decade before called *The Whole Duty of a Woman* (author unknown). And the recipe is not for a *Yorkshire* pudding; it's for a *dripping* pudding. The anonymous cook tells us to make a pancake batter (which is all a Yorkshire pudding batter is), to pour it into a wide pan already containing some dripping from a roasting joint, and then to 'put the Pan and Batter under a Shoulder of Mutton instead of a Dripping-pan, keeping frequently shaking it by the Handle'. So, it turns out that there is no Yorkshire providence and no roast beef. So how did a dripping pudding become associated with Yorkshire? The answer is unclear, but I believe it is because of the way the people of God's Own Country partook of it. Eaten as a starter with gravy – rabbit gravy was a particular favourite in some parts – or sometimes jam, the

SUET

Suet is the most commonly used fat in steamed and boiled puddings, and it seems to have been used to enrich puddings ever since their inception. It is the compacted, flaky fat found cushioning the kidneys of a mammal, and it is usually derived from beef. With Britain being a beef-eating country, there was plenty of it about, so it was cheap; but it was also good, because although it does enrich a pudding, it doesn't impart any obvious flavour. Puddings are best when made with proper fresh suet: your butcher will give you some free, or for mere pennies. Dorothy Hartley was of the opinion that when making a meat suet pudding, one should use the suet of the animal found in the filling to make the pastry. Lamb suet is good, but it does impart a definitely lamby flavour. Excess fresh suet can be frozen for up to three months. Indeed, before the days of cheap refrigeration it seems that sometimes less-than-perfect suet was being used, because Eliza Acton makes the point that '[t]he perfect sweetness of suet and milk should be especially attended to before they are mixed into a pudding, as nothing can be more offensive than the first when it is overkept.'

The answer to this issue came in the form of packaged, rendered suet, the best-known brand in Britain being Atora, who opened their first factory in Manchester in 1893. It had a long shelf-life and was very easy to use. Vegan suet is also produced, and although it tastes fine, the vast majority of it is made from unsustainably sourced palm fat (but not all, so it is worth shopping around). According to the back page of the 1932 edition of *The Recipe Book of 'Atora'*, their packaged suet 'has been supplied to all of the Polar Expeditions, and has improved the cooking of hundreds of thousands of British housewives'. Atora advertised its suet as a pure and nourishing source of fat, and even provided medical evidence for its essential role in the proper development of children, informing us that the 'young human being requires a continuous supply of this substance'. I'm not sure it could be marketed in that way today!

THE RECIPE BOOK
OF
"ATORA"
Refined BEEF SUET

Nearly 100 Recipes.

Economical!
Helpful!
Delicious!
Nourishing!

Sole Proprietors & Manufacturers

HUGON & CO., Ltd., Manchester.

hungry diners would fill up on cheap, delicious pudding and then eat less of the expensive meat. Parents would say to their children, 'Yan 'at eeats maist Pudden gets maist meeat.'[1] As we moved away from spit-roasting joints of meat in front of fires to baking them in ovens, the Yorkshire pudding moved too; now it was baked in a large rectangular tray in a brisk oven, records Peter Brears in *Traditional Food in Yorkshire* (2014), 'the batter rising to a high, crisp rim, with a shallower deeply rippled centre'.

Controversies have always surrounded the making of them, and what does – and does not – constitute a proper Yorkshire pudding. This really came to a head in Leeds in the April of 1970, when the Great Yorkshire Pudding Contest was held, pitting chefs and home cooks against each other to bake their best efforts. The winner was a chef from Hong Kong called Tin Sung Chan. His glorious pudding rose high, was crisp around the edges, and was soft in the middle. However, the award was quickly disputed because apparently Mr Chan's batter had too high a ratio of eggs to flour and it hadn't been allowed to rest – the flour had been folded into the milk and eggs and the batter immediately tipped into its tin. Then – shock, horror – the secret to Mr Chan's success was identified as the mysterious *tai luk* sauce, an addition disallowed in a true Yorkshire pudding mixture. *Guardian* journalist Michael Parkin called it '[a]n arrogant soufflé of a podin [*sic*] inflated far beyond its culinary station'. Ouch.

Poor Mr Chan, he had never made a Yorkshire pudding before and had been talked into taking part in the competition by his boss as a bit of promotion for the restaurant at which he worked. He was forced to make a statement via his employer telling everyone that he hadn't expected to win, and that he would not be making any more puddings in future. This was reported by Michael Parkin a week later in an article entitled 'End of threat to Yorkshire'. And the *tai luk* sauce? It turned out to be a little culinary joke, meaning 'mainland'. This was realised by Jane Grigson, who was informed of the fact after traipsing around every Asian grocery store she passed trying to hunt it down; it was just 'an amiable joke at the expense of Yorkshire patriotism'. Well, that backfired.

Custard Puddings

Custard-based puddings are very delicate, so it's quite surprising to find their origins in the boiling pot, where they were called quaking or shaking puddings. They were usually stabilised with some flour, breadcrumbs or ground almonds. They had to be turned out into serving dishes most deftly, as any hesitation would surely create a split. Sir Kenelm Digby's 1669 recipe is the earliest I can find, and it is a rich mixture of milk, egg yolks, bread, sack and bone marrow. Often these jiggly puddings were served prickled like hedgehogs with sharp almond slivers. They were quickly adapted to oven baking in the Georgian era; there had already been a long-established habit of baking custards in tarts since the Middle Ages, but these puddings were cooked in dishes sat in hot water. These baked custards were set only by the action of egg, and they have remained a firm favourite ever since; set custard cups, crème brûlée and crème caramel are examples of their descendants. Some quaking puddings remained in their cloths and moulds and contained not just custard but pieces of sponge cake, as well as dried and candied fruits to make chancellor's or diplomat's pudding – puds rarely made these days.

There is a crossover here with bread puddings, because Manchester pudding is a custard breadcrumb mixture baked in a puff-pastry case lined with jam. It is first described in the Victorian era. From that came queen of puddings, one of the best of all British puddings; here the same bread-and-custard base is baked in a dish until set, spread gingerly with a good, tart jam, then topped with meringue and baked again until the snowy peaks have turned golden brown. Extremely sweet and extremely good.

Transparent Puddings

Possibly the most obscure order of sweet puddings is the transparent puddings, which are rarely made today, except for one quite famous regional speciality. They are a very rich mixture of egg, sugar and melted butter, poured into a dish or a puff-pastry case. '[B]ake it in a moderate Oven half an hour, and it will cut light and clear', wrote Elizabeth Raffald in *The Experienced English Housekeeper* (1769), hence the name. They first appear in the seventeenth century, and they were made very fancy with the addition of candied and dried fruits and chopped roasted nuts – delicious but teeth-achingly sweet. In the first half of the nineteenth century, the sweetmeats were swapped for a spreading of raspberry jam, the toasted nuts for some ground almonds, and in doing so the Bakewell pudding was born. They are still made in their thousands in the Derbyshire town that gave its name, and at least three establishments reckon to be the ones selling the true and original pudding. As far as I can see, transparent puddings are the only main group that doesn't have its origins in pudding cloths or moulds.

By the end of the nineteenth century, a multitude of puddings were now available; they could be delicate and quivering custards or 'solid' roly-polies, but while technology gave us cloths, moulds, range ovens and steamers, no single cooking method won out, and you chose the best method for the task. Everyone ate pudding at some point in the year; no one turned their nose up at even the most basic – only a fool would turn down a portion of jam roly-poly and custard. A true democratic British institution of which we should be proud, pudding was, and is, for all.

Jelly and Blancmange

In the eighteenth century, British cuisine was moving away from the opulent royal-court-style French cookery associated with the Tudors and the Stuarts. Puddings were emblematic of this: they were simple to make (though not necessarily cheap) and they were usually made from just a few ingredients. But in the latter half of the eighteenth century, another type of food would become considered a pudding, yet was definitely posh: jelly, blancmange and flummery. Jellies had begun life in the Tudor period as leaches, a soft-set gelatine food that was usually sliced up or served in bowls. Blancmange appears in *Forme of Cury* (*c*.1390) as a chicken, rice and almond dish, but from around 1600, it morphed into a sweet almond jelly, a very different creature. Flummeries were starch-set jellies, the starch extracted by simmering cracked cereal grains in water, then straining the liquid, flavouring it and allowing it to set. By the eighteenth century blancmange and flummery had converged into a sweetened almond milk jelly, the terms essentially interchangeable.

All three of these foods were set either with gelatine extracted from calves' feet, or from isinglass, which was derived from the bones and swim bladders of certain fish, the best being sourced from sturgeon. Extraction and purification were laborious, energy-consuming processes: hours simmering and several bouts of skimming, straining

COOKING IN A CLOTH: SOME COOKERY TIPS FROM THE EXPERTS

To truly understand the pudding, I believe one must, at least once, boil one in a cloth. Eliza Acton tells us in *Modern Cookery for Private Families* that a batter or suet pudding 'is much lighter when boiled in a cloth and allowed full room to swell, than when confined to a mould', and that 'plum puddings are less dry when cooked in cloth'. Cloth-cooked puddings are, quite simply, the best. It is easy to do using a large square of muslin or cheesecloth, or a good-sized tea towel (or indeed a clean pillowcase): 'take Care your Cloth is very clean, dip it in boiling Water, and Flour it well, and give your Cloth a shake,' wrote Elizabeth Raffald; this is the equivalent of buttering and flouring a cake tin. When the pudding has finished cooking, you must turn it out, says Raffald, 'very carefully, for very often a light Pudding is broken in turning out'. Once sat in its serving dish, 'the pudding should be sent to table as expeditiously as possible ... or it will become heavy.'

The Family Plum Pudding.

MODERN MODE OF SERVING DISHES.

S 1. Jelly of two colours.   T 1. Raspberry Cream.   U 1. Centre Dish of Various Fruits.
V 1. Trifle.   W 1. Strawberries au naturel in ornamental Flowerpot.

and clarifying. But by the 1760s cooks were so adept at making gelatine stocks that they set quite stiff, thereby providing, for the first time, the potential for setting jellies in moulds with some height to them.

Elizabeth Raffald was the pioneer, and she devised a large number of exciting and theatrical jelly and flummery centrepieces, all of which are detailed in *The Experienced English Housekeeper*. Her *pièce de résistance* was her 'Solomon's Temple in Flummery', a four-cornered obelisk with tapering towers and a tall and slender central monolith that, once turned out, had to be made stable by inserting a flower down its length. The stress of turning out the thing from its porcelain mould must have been immense. Elizabeth also devised other notable creations, including 'bacon and eggs in flummery' and 'cribbage cards in flummery'. They were eye-catching, fun and very costly to make. When she left domestic service and moved to Manchester, she started a business selling her gelatine creations to housewives who didn't have the equipment, or staff, to make them in-house. It is in her aforementioned 1769 book that, for the first time, a set gelatine dessert is called a pudding. Elizabeth has a jelly version of a transparent pudding – a mix of candied fruit, dried stone fruit and roasted nuts suspended in a refreshing lemon jelly. These first moulds were made from very thin porcelain, but towards the end of the century beautifully shaped and detailed copper moulds were produced. Their thinness combined with the excellent conductive properties of copper made these set puddings much easier to turn out; and because they were made in moulds, they were made honorary puddings.

Into the nineteenth century, set desserts began to diverge into two different sorts: those that were attainable to the middle classes, and those available only to the very wealthy as another wave of opulent French cookery hit the royal courts. At the helm was Antonin Carême, who at one point was chef to the Prince Regent, but other French chefs, such as Louis-Eustache Ude, Alexis Soyer and Charles Elmé Francatelli, devised ever more expensive and complex moulds: one jelly was made by filling hollowed oranges with alternate stripes of orange jelly and white blancmange, another was a crystal-clear champagne jelly shimmering with gold leaf. Whoever was eating jelly and blancmange at this time, they were certainly not giving it to children.

At the same time, set desserts were being made by the middle classes – a tier of British society that was (and possibly still is) most competitive from a social mobility point of view – with the production of the first preparatory isinglass in 1824. Now housewives without the knowledge, skill or inclination to extract gelatine from animals could buy some at their local grocer's shop. The uptake was slow at first, but by the 1880s the gelatine was extracted and purified very well, had no gluiness, and even came in a range of colours and flavours. Cheaper moulds made

LEMON
RASPBERRY
ORANGE
CHERRY
PINEAPPLE
STRAWBERRY
RIZINE Cos.
Fruit Jelly Flakes.
SEE OTHER SIDE.

FREEMAN'S PU
MADE
IN
FIVE
MINUTES
ALMOND · LEMON · VANILLA · C
FANCY BOXES 3 PACKET
PURE WHOLESOME & NUTRITIOU
FREEMAN & HILDYARD. DO

DING POWDER
A CHILD
CAN
MAKE THEM
ONLY
ADDITION
MILK
&
SUGAR
COLATE · PEACH · NECTARINE
D., SIX PACKETS 1S. EACH.
LAVOURS DELICATE & DELICIOUS.
R RD. BOROUGH LONDON. S.E.

from tinned steel were introduced, meaning that jelly and blancmange were a standard fancy dessert at the dinner parties of the lower-middle classes.

The working classes too were tucking into set desserts at the turn of the twentieth century, but they were set with much cheaper starch, and it is here we see the first cornflour-set blancmanges, and semolina or ground-rice moulded puddings. It is at this time that, for me, set moulded foods can be truly called puddings. First of all they were all made in moulds like regular puddings, but more importantly, they were now enjoyed by everyone. Okay, some may be made with bits of gold leaf bobbing about in them, and others with starch, milk and sugar, but they were there in some shape or form, wobbling away on everyone's dinner tables.

PUDDING AND IDENTITY

THE BOND BETWEEN the British and their puddings is a strong one, but between the mid-eighteenth and mid-twentieth centuries it was almost palpable, and one pudding stood head and shoulders above all others: the proud, round, plum pudding. Like many others, this pudding was not eaten for afters at first, but with meat, especially roast beef. It was a meal that displayed Britain's superiority and strength. It was the national dish. The home-grown beef symbolised cutting-edge farming and agricultural techniques, of which the British considered themselves leaders; and it was combined with a British pudding made with exotic ingredients sourced from its ever-expanding empire.

The precursor to plum pudding is medieval, a pottage made of broth, meat, spices, dried fruits and breadcrumbs. Being chock-full of expensive ingredients, it was a feasting dish. By the early seventeenth century, recipes appear for plum pottage, but it evolves at this time too, and is cooked in a pudding cloth, the beef no longer part of

Jas Gillray des.

The Plumb-pudding in dange
"the great Globe itself and all which it inher

_ State Epicures taking un Petit Souper.
s too small to satisfy such insatiable appetites.
vide Mr W—d—s eccentricities my Political Regrth

the pudding mixture. Now the pottage was a pudding, its popularity soared, and a century later it was a part of England's culinary landscape. It was the pudding that incoming German King George I requested at his first Christmas dinner as British monarch in 1714. He knew it would ingratiate him; whether he really enjoyed it or not is a different matter, of course. The plum pud had become such a common feature by 1805 that it was used in a political cartoon, by James Gillray, entitled *The Plumb-Pudding in Danger*, to highlight the issues the country was having with import and export during the Napoleonic Wars. The cartoon shows a lanky William Pitt and squat Napoleon Bonaparte slicing up and portioning out the globe, which is depicted as a huge, yielding plum pudding. After Napoleon's defeat at Waterloo in 1815, the British Empire was able to trade freely, receiving imports from both the East and West Indies and its other colonies. It's worth pointing out that despite the range of ingredients that have historically gone into a plum pudding, no one seems to have ever included plums (or rather prunes – 'plum' was a byword for any dried stone fruit). By the way, there are no figs in figgy pudding either.

Plum pudding became associated with Christmas because it was a feasting dish. Of course, a special enriched version was made, it being the most special time of year, but it only became indelibly imprinted on the nation's psyche as a Christmas tradition when Charles Dickens included it

Mrs Cratchit brings in the pudding.

Mrs. Cratchit entered— flushed, but smiling proudly—with the pudding, like a speckled cannon-ball, and bedight with Christmas holly stuck in the top.

in his best-seller *A Christmas Carol* (1843); his description of the poor Cratchit family's rather austere pudding is wonderfully evocative and romantic:

> Hallo! A great deal of steam! The pudding was out of the copper. A smell like washing-day! That was the cloth. A smell like an eating-house, and a pastry-cook's next door to each other, with a laundress's next door to that! That was the pudding. In half a minute Mrs. Cratchit entered: flushed, but smiling proudly: with the pudding, like a speckled cannon-ball, so hard and bedight with Christmas holly stuck on top.

Having made several in my time, I must say that he does rather nail the spectacle.

Dickens uses the pudding in another way: to cause offence. Before his dramatic change of heart, Ebenezer Scrooge knew exactly how to ruin his nephew's annoyingly upbeat Christmas cheer:

> "If I could work my will," said Scrooge, indignantly, "every idiot who goes about with 'Merry Christmas' on his lips, should be boiled with his own pudding, and buried with a stake of holly through his heart. He should!"

Eliza Acton has two recipes for Christmas pudding in her *Modern Cookery for Private Families*, printed two years after Dickens' novella. They differ from other plum puddings in that they have a little more fruit and a glug or two of Christmas booze, but they are nowhere near as rich and dark as modern Christmas puddings.

By the middle of the Victorian era, everybody was enjoying a plum pudding at least once a year; even the workhouse poor were given it at Christmas and on other important celebration days. An article in the *Supplement to the Illustrated London News* of 1850 puts it thus:

> While the twelfth cake is more an aristocratic type, the Plum pudding is a national symbol. It does not represent a class or caste, but the bulk of the English nation. There is not a man, woman or child raised above what the French would call *proletaires* that does not expect a taste of plum pudding of some sort or another on Christmas Day.

Have an EMPIRE Xmas Pudding

This is How to Make it.

Take 1 breakfastcupful of each of the following eight ingredients:— Canadian flour, Australian or South African raisins, Australian sultanas, Australian currants, Demerara sugar, chopped mixed peel, English or Scottish beef suet, breadcrumbs. Also 1 English cooking apple, 4 to 6 eggs (Home laid), 1 teaspoonful pudding spice (Indian), 1 wineglassful Jamaica rum, sufficient milk to mix, grated rind and juice of one lemon. One English 3d. bit for luck!

Mix well. Place in greased basin. Cover with greaseproof paper; tie on cloth and steam or boil 6 to 8 hours.

Here you have a quite simple recipe. It will make as delicious a plum pudding as you have ever tasted. And you will enjoy it all the more if you remember that, by using Empire fruit to make it, you give a helping hand to the thousands of British settlers Overseas—most of them ex-Service men and their families—by whom that fruit is grown.

Buy EMPIRE GOODS

ASK—IS IT BRITISH?

ISSUED BY THE EMPIRE MARKETING BOARD

In the latter half of the nineteenth century, superstitious traditions began to sneak in, such as the adding of trinkets: a coin, ring and thimble. Stir Up Sunday was appropriated from the Anglican Church by the Edwardians as a day to stir up the pudding mixture: everyone had to have a stir or add an ingredient and make a Christmas wish. Some said that it had to contain thirteen ingredients, representing Jesus and his twelve disciples. This may have been true for a time, but puddings became richer from the 1930s after the creation of King George V's 'Empire Pudding'. Made of seventeen ingredients, each from a different dominion, it was a vain attempt to keep the national pride going at a time when the empire was falling apart. Empire became Commonwealth, but for the Christmas pudding, the Empire Pudding set a precedent and they remained forever rich (Second World War aside, that is). Delia Smith, never one for frivolities, puts eighteen ingredients into her Christmas pudding recipe in her *Complete Cookery Course* (1982), including a kilo of dried fruit, four tots of rum, and half a pint each of stout and barley wine. If, like me, you find modern Christmas puddings a bit much, I take this opportunity to advise you to seek out a nineteenth-century recipe.

The igniting of a brandy-drenched pudding is one of the few examples of dinnertime theatre in which we still partake, and it is described wonderfully by Agatha Christie in her short story 'The Adventure of the Christmas Pudding' (1960): 'On a silver dish the Christmas pudding reposed in its glory. A large football of a pudding, a piece of holly stuck in it like a triumphant flag and glorious flames of blue and red rising round it. There was a cheer and cries of "Ooh-ah".' A rousing spectacle indeed.

Of course, puddings of many other sorts crop up in English literature, and there are almost too many to mention. The vast majority of the time, they appear in children's stories, such as Beatrix Potter's *The Roly-Poly Pudding* (1908), later published as *The Tale of Samuel Whiskers*. It is the story of a very naughty kitten who gets captured by the rat Samuel Whiskers, who, together with his wife, ties up the little cat and rolls him in pudding pastry, presumably to boil him. In the wonderfully absurdist *The Magic Pudding* (1918) by Norman Lindsay, Albert, a magical steak and kidney pudding with the ability to regenerate, must escape pudding thieves, lest he is captured and forever imprisoned. In the twenty-first century J. K. Rowling makes sure the pudding takes pride of place in the Hogwarts Christmas feast, a school where all of the best of the old traditions are kept alive.

However, we mustn't forget who was most likely making the family's often twice-daily dose of pudding, and Charlotte Brontë includes the activity of pudding-making as one of life's drudgeries for the housewife to endure in *Jane Eyre* (1847):

> Women are supposed to be very calm generally: but women feel just as men feel; they need exercise for their faculties, and a field for their efforts as much as their brothers do; they suffer from too rigid a restraint, too absolute a stagnation, precisely as men would suffer, and it is narrow-minded in their more privileged fellow-creatures to say that they ought to confine themselves to making puddings and knitting stockings…

Puddings are used in humour too, such as in Robert Burns' famous *Address to a Haggis*:

> Fair fa' your honest, sonsie face,
> Great chieftain o' the pudding-race!
> Aboon them a' ye tak your place,
> Painch, tripe, or thairm:
> Weel are ye wordy o'a grace
> As lang's my arm.

Here, Burns purposefully provides an overly elaborate and gushing toast to a most humble foodstuff. But he is half-joking of course, because everyone *was* proud of their iconic national dish.

With such a long history, it's perhaps no surprise that puddings appear in folkloric stories, most pleasingly in the tale of the Dragon of Knucker Hole. The Knucker, a type of water dragon, after terrorising the people and livestock of the village of Lyminster in Sussex, is defeated by the brave Jack, who gallantly serves the dragon a Sussex pudding so large that it has to be pulled into its lair on a cart. The Knucker scoffs it in one go, and demands another. Jack dutifully obeys, and the second is promptly devoured. However, the puddings slowly expand in the dragon's stomach and it slumps forward, the victim of a carb coma, if you will. Jack beheads the Knucker and returns to the village triumphant. A reminder to us all that a second helping of pudding is not always a good idea.

Puddings may not always be pretty, but people do take pride – quite rightly – in the puddings of their childhood or their region, despite most of these links being vague and the differences between them only slight. Take the following pairs of sponge puddings: a Portland pudding is flavoured with dried fruit and candied peel, whereas a Helston pudding is flavoured with dried fruit, candied peel *and* nutmeg; a Berkeley pudding has lemon zest and mixed spice, but a Canterbury pudding has lemon zest and brandy. These tiny differences are small enough to be essentially negligible, yet tempers fray should anyone omit a spice or add a handful of dried fruit or whatever. It happens with other puddings too. For example, what is the difference between a chancellor's and a diplomat's pudding? The former is a steamed pudding of cake pieces, dried and candied fruit, and custard, served piping hot. Delicious. A diplomat pudding is exactly the same, but is eaten cold. There are several theories as to how this proliferation of puddings and their associated nomenclature happened: first, it made a pudding stand out from the others, and made it more memorable, especially if the recipe was to appear in print; secondly, with the postal system, recipes were exchanged by letter, the writers probably wanting to communicate the favourite pudding, or the most common type of pudding, in their town or village; lastly, it was a good way of attracting visitors and holidaymakers to cafés and bakeries. Food historian and writer Regula Ysewijn suspects that the latter happened in Bakewell, and I am sure she is correct, because it is very much a money-spinner for the town today.

MILK PUDDINGS

Just the thought of tucking into a milk pudding is likely to have you salivating for one of two opposing reasons: either they are a wonderful and comforting ambrosia, or they make you feel queasy, triggering memories of sloppy school semolina and sago.

Puddings of something starchy mixed with milk or cream and a few aromatics go back to time immemorial, and no other pudding has adapted so well to advances in pudding technology and changes in taste and circumstance as rice pudding; so much so, in fact, it has lapped itself. It began life, or rather its precursor began life, as a medieval pottage made especially for fasting days, and it is made by cooking rice in almond milk until it 'be stondying', i.e. thick enough that a spoon will stand up in it without falling over. It might be a Lenten dish, but don't be mistaken, it is not a humble one: rice, almonds and sugar were very expensive imports. In the era of the Stuarts, cooked, sweet rice mixtures were now prepared inside lengths of gut and made with ingredients such as dates, sugar, cream and

DELIGHTS FOR THE OLD AND YOUNG.
Directions for the above are all contained within this book.

saffron. I have made these early rice puddings in the past and I must say they are very delicious. There are recipes for rice puddings cooked in cloths and basins too, and recipes using both cooking methods crop up in Hannah Glasse's *The Art of Cookery Made Plain and Easy* (1747). A glut of recipes for baked rice puddings can be found in eighteenth-century cookery books, correlating with the advent of the cast-iron range cooker. They were often baked in puff pastry, using rice that had already been cooked. The type of baked rice pudding made by cooking rice from raw in milk or cream and sugar came in the nineteenth century. Slow-baked puddings made for excellent home economy, sitting at the bottom of the oven, ticking away as the main meal was being cooked on the hot top shelves. This is a classic baked rice pudding, made in a shallow dish with a golden skin on top, the pinnacle of rice pudding cookery, in my humble opinion.

In the Victorian era milk puddings become part of a group called nursery puddings: cheap, plain and therefore fit for children. The science of nutrition and dietetics was being taken very seriously in the early twentieth century, and as milk puddings were considered very wholesome, they quickly became an integral part of school meals. All good so far, except for the opposing factor: budgetary constraint. Coming in on budget meant the puddings were thin and sloppy and cooked quickly on the hob: milk puddings had become institutionalised. And so we have ended up at the beginning: rice pudding as a pottage, a sweet soup. These modern, plain preparatory puddings lack one important quality compared to their medieval ancestor: they will never 'be stondying'.

The trauma of being forced to eat overcooked and gelatinous 'frogspawn' tapioca pudding has the power to nauseate people of a certain age today, decades after their ordeal. One of these people was Jane Grigson, who had carried with her a hatred of them ever since her years at boarding school. She plucked up the courage to bake a proper rice pudding. She cooked it, she ate it, and she concluded that 'a rice pudding must be flavoured with a vanilla pod or cinnamon stick, it must be cooked long and slowly, it must be eaten with plenty of double cream. Like so many English dishes, it has been wrecked by meanness and lack of thought.' She perfectly expresses the way simple and honest cookery can be hijacked by stinginess or corner-cutting. Good, simple foods demand a cook with an eye for detail, a deftness of touch and an appreciation of good-quality ingredients.

Sometimes a consensus regarding what does and what does not make a particular pudding cannot be reached. Take spotted dick, for example. For me, it's a mixture of flour, suet, currants, milk, sugar and lemon zest poured into a mould and steamed. However, a reader informed me that I had actually made a *song* pudding; for it to qualify as a spotted dick, the mixture should have been boiled in a cloth. Others say it must be cylindrical in shape, boiled or steamed and served in slices, yet others declare that's actually an Exeter dick, not a spotted dick. No one can agree on what the 'dick' means either: options include a retraction of the word 'puddick', a dialect word for pudding; or a corruption of 'spotted dog'. Others reckon it might just mean dough. The less important the differences, the more animated we become defending the honour of our favourite local or childhood puddings, and it is testament to our love for them.

SULTANA PUDDING.

PUDDING FOR DESSERT

IN THE MID-NINETEENTH century a new way of dining was introduced, and it came from the very opulent royal Russian courts. It was called service *à la russe*, or Russian service, and it meant that single dishes were brought out over several, separate courses one at a time, as opposed to the old French service where lots of dishes came ready laid out on the dining table. At first, everyone was rather confused by the whole thing, there were far too many courses, and meals took hours. But as a consequence of this change in service, dishes began to separate, almost like chromatography: soup and fish came first (this had been the way for centuries), but then came the very savoury foods, such as richly roasted meats, cutlets and fricassees, then plainer roasts and lighter poultry, shellfish or eggs in aspic, and soufflés. Sweet foods like pastries, jellies, gateaux, fritters and puddings were served as entremets, and if it was a particularly fancy meal, these foods would be split into entremets and desserts, hence the pudding became detached from its traditional savoury balancing companion.

SAUCES FOR PUDDINGS

A good pudding requires a good accompaniment, and today we reach most commonly for the custard. This might be made from custard powder, or bought in a tin, tub or carton from the supermarket. If you take a look at the ingredients list of any of these things, you will see that none contain egg yolks – the one ingredient custard purists would say has to be in a proper custard sauce. It also goes by the name *crème anglaise*, not because the sauce was thought to have been conceived in England, but because its inhabitants loved it so much – not unlike the people of Yorkshire and their Yorkshire pudding. Some prefer the contrast of ice cream, which is frozen custard anyway. Of course, if the pudding is very rich, cream is the perfect companion, and it's what I always serve with sticky toffee pudding. The only time we veer from this is at Christmastime, when the brandy butter, which used to go by the name 'hard sauce', is eaten with the Christmas pud.

And that's where we stop, but we are missing out on a whole diversity of forgotten pudding sauces. Rich sauces go well with plain puddings: sweet, or pudding, sauce was a combination of equal amounts of sweet or fortified wine, sugar and melted butter, stirred until the sugar dissolved. Other sauces were based on traditional butter sauce, usually served with fish or boiled vegetables. The sweet version had most or all of the milk swapped for booze: punch sauce was flavoured with orange and lemon rind and juice, white wine, brandy and rum, and, of course, plenty of sugar.

Fruity sauces made from sieved redcurrants or raspberries, sweetened with sugar and thickened with arrowroot, were commonly served with custard puddings like quaking or bread and butter pudding. A simpler and cheaper version was jam sauce, made with a preserve rather than fresh fruit. It doesn't stop there: there's currant sauce, sweet egg sauce (using hard-boiled eggs; not sure about that one), lemon sauce, German pudding sauce … the list goes on and on. A great variety of puddings required a great variety of sauces. They might seem a bit much today, but they can elevate a simple plain suet or sponge pudding into a most indulgent dessert.

Not all dinners were grand affairs, and during the week, when just the family was eating, the entremets were heavily reduced in number: a plain cabinet pudding and an apple tart may have made up their 'afters'. There was luncheon too, of course, consisting of a light savoury dish and one simple sweet pudding – something not too expensive and that didn't take up too much of the kitchen staff's time, like a plum duff or roly-poly.

Of the entremets and dessert dishes, puddings now made up the majority – and why not? They were cheap, and everyone loved them dearly. People became so used to having pudding at the end of a meal that the phrase 'What's for dessert?' became 'What's for pudding?'; using the word pudding to mean desserts of all types is upper class in its origins. This transition is very clear in the wonderful *Everybody's Pudding Book* by Georgiana Hill (1862), and in the introduction we can see how pudding, or the pudding course, is beginning to encompass other sweet foods. Georgiana wrestles with what types of foods should be included in her book: 'Besides puddings, tarts, and pies', she says, obviously secure in the idea that sweet pastry products were now pudding, 'I have introduced custards, not that they can be considered as coming under the category of pastry but on account of their being essential additions to many kinds of tarts and fruit-puddings,' adding, '[f]ritters, omelets, and other entremets, I have also given, because they are quickly made.'

She also emphasises to the reader (and her staff) that simple puddings are not to be sniffed at and that puddings can be enjoyed at every occasion: 'at first sight some of the dishes may not be thought to be of a recherché description ... and while the humblest of the preparations presented in these pages will, upon trial, be found to have merited their well-established reputations for homely excellence, the more elegant amongst them also possess the one great recommendation of being within the reach of Amphitryons [i.e. kings] and housekeepers of the most moderate means.' Her June puddings include gooseberry tart, quaking pudding, lemon cheesecakes, *pain perdu*, a 'cheap bread pudding' and Reform Club pudding.

Eating a lunch and a dinner featuring puddings and entremets on a daily basis was still in the realm of the well-off right into the Edwardian period, but puddings did begin to trickle down into the mealtimes of the lower classes. Puddings made sense: they were straight-forward to make and often required mainly store-cupboard ingredients. They filled and they warmed, a most important factor before the advent of cheap and reliable central heating. A cheap pudding could be served up at a time when men came home from work to take their luncheon. As usual, the precise proportion of expensive ingredients was dependent upon one's home economics; a simple boiled suet pudding of flour, suet, breadcrumbs, perhaps an egg, and sweetened with just some currants or a simple jam

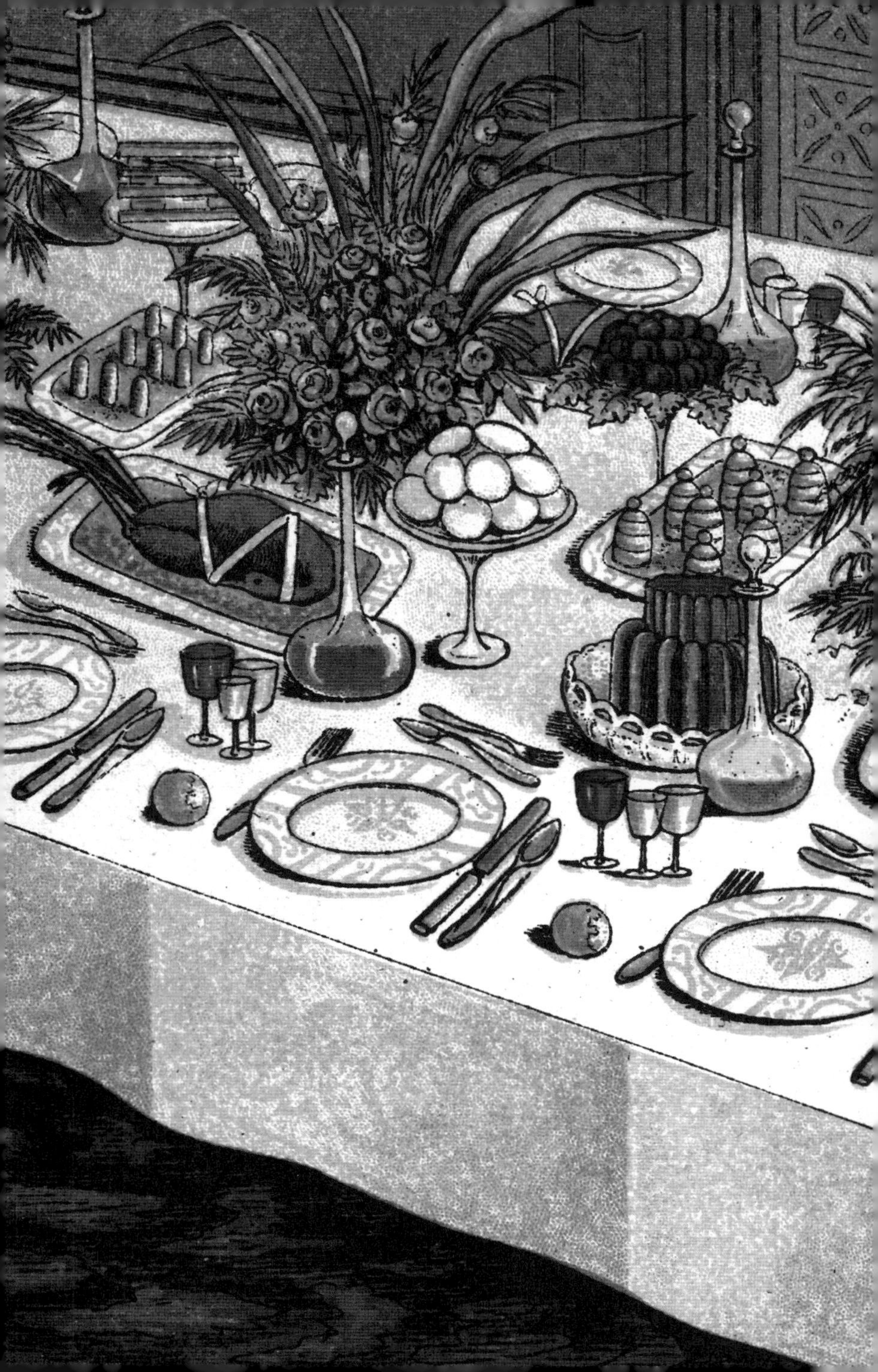

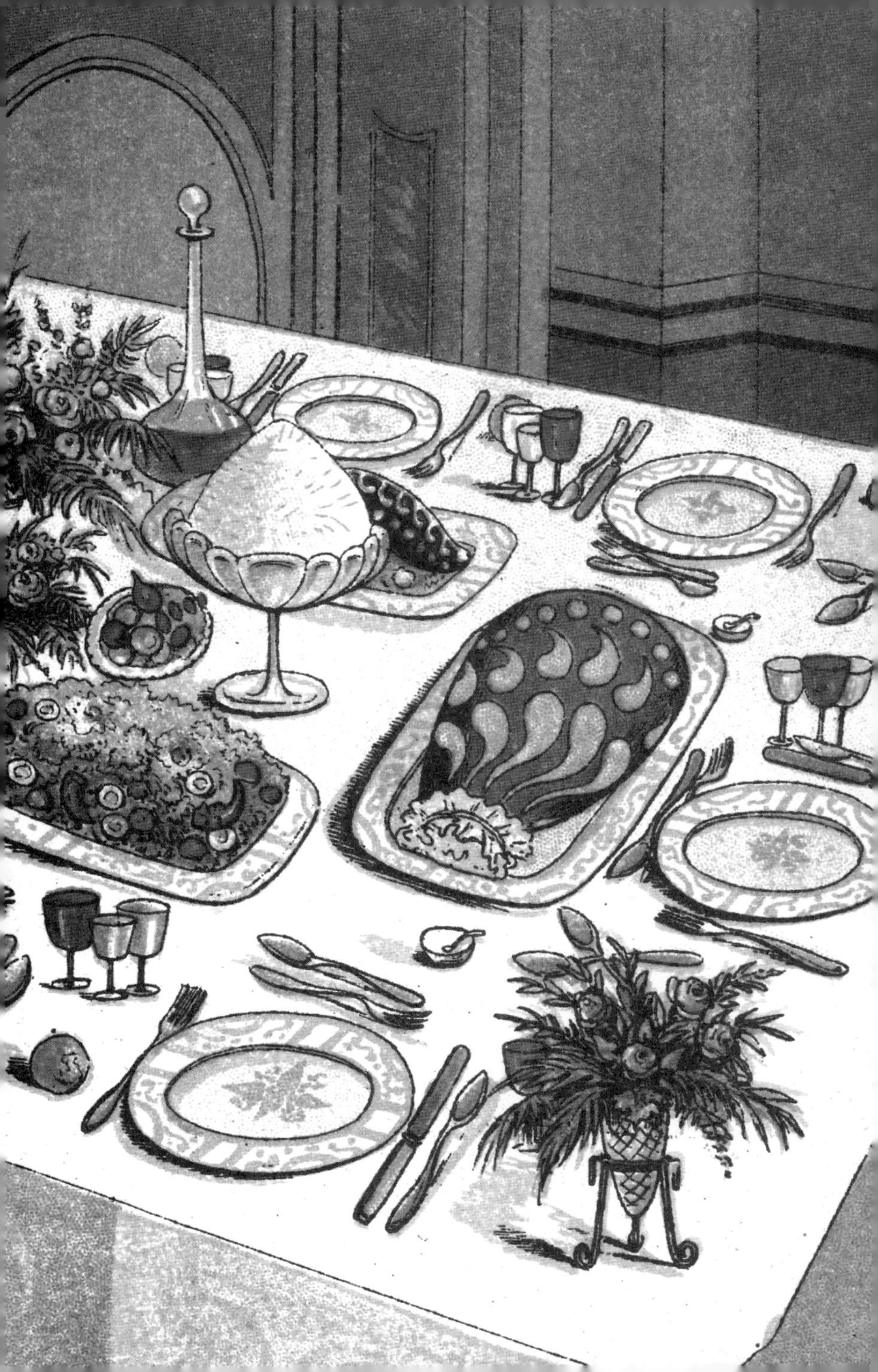

sauce would be typical. Refined sugars wouldn't be used in large amounts, but cheaper brown sugar, golden syrup or dark treacle were used instead, and let's face it, they are much more flavoursome and texturally interesting than white caster sugar.

In the 1920s things changed: the middle classes, who had been enjoying the benefit of having staff to aid the housewife in her duties for a good 150 years or so, suddenly found themselves without help. This was partially due to economic reasons, but also because many women who had been domestic servants worked in the munitions factories during the Great War and had seen that a more independent life was possible, away from the oppressive drudgery of domestic service. Without skilled help, homemade puddings became less complex in nature. Many women found pudding cloths difficult to use; however, cheap tin moulds, and then aluminium ones in the 1930s, saved the day to some degree. These were designed to be easy to use; some came with their own lids and metal clips, fiddly string or cloth lids now no longer required. Others came with a central hole and they were more often steamed than boiled, meaning their contents would cook quicker, reducing the cooking time further. With the common use of chemical raising agents, the steam pudding came into its own. So, in the end, despite a drop in skills and domestic help, the ever-adaptable pudding still managed to remain top-ranking, the perfect end to a meal. A negative consequence of this change, however, is that pudding diversity dropped because the vast majority of housewives cooked just a limited repertoire of recipes.

With the onset of the Second World War, Britain was plunged into a prolonged bout of food rationing, one that was much more austere compared to rationing in the Great War. It took housewives out of the home and into the workplace. When the war was over, many housewives did not want this particular aspect of wartime life to stop, and after the war, more women decided to work. Unfortunately, they were still expected to do the vast majority – if not all – of the child-rearing, home-making and cooking. There followed a swift change in kitchen technology, when dirty cast-iron fireplaces were exchanged for clean gas ovens and hobs. Steamed sponges hung on, but most puddings were baked in the oven (alongside the main meal) or cooked in a saucepan, and were more likely to be made at the weekend, when there was more time to hand. The pudding had to adapt again, and any that took a long time to boil or steam were not conducive to modern living, with both parents out of the house.

In response to these societal changes, the food industry produced a range of preparatory and packet foods. They hastened the cooking process, especially useful in the preparation of weekday meals, when families still expected a pudding after dinner: tinned tapioca or macaroni puddings, tinned fruit, tinned evaporated milk and tinned

"Hullo Kiddies
I've been shopping!"
BIRD'S CUSTARD
Creamy & Egg-like
BIRD'S CUSTARD POWDER
"PUDDENA"
MADE ONLY BY BIRD'S
MAKES LIGHT TASTY PUDDINGS
It's a Powder
BIRD'S CRYSTAL JELLY LEMON Powder
and Dissolves Instantly!
BIRD'S EGG SUBSTITUTE
BIRD'S CONCENTRATED EGG SUBSTITUTE
BIRD'S BLANC-MANGE POWDER
Made in a moment
Ready flavoured.
BIRD'S BLANC-MANGE POWDER
BIRD'S "SPONGIE"
A SPONGE MIXTURE FOR MAKING SWISS ROLL SANDWICH, ETC.

pie fillings. There was even a range of (if I remember correctly, very delicious) boil-in-the-tin sponge puddings made by Heinz. There too were the now standard packet jellies, cornflour blancmanges and custard powders. Angel Delight displaced syllabubs and fools, and Instant Whip even managed to displace cream. In the 1970s fridges and freezers became affordable, and we began to receive a range of frozen desserts and puddings: ice cream, once the fanciest of all the desserts, now an accompaniment to lowly, common puddings! What would our ancestors have made of that? There was Arctic roll, there was Wall's Viennetta. Some puddings just required defrosting: Supermousses, cheesecakes and pavlovas. It was a frozen-food revolution, and it caused the number of traditionally made puddings to drop yet again.

In the 1980s, yet another phase of fancy French cookery encroached, this time in the form of *nouvelle cuisine*. Now puddings were being threatened with extinction: people preferred to tuck into sugar-laden factory-processed preparations, or they were shunned by food snobs, embarrassed by the Great British Pudding, an old-fashioned blob of stodge. But some were flying the flag for puddings, most notably the members of the Pudding Club, established in 1985 in Micklefield in the Cotswolds. They were 'determined not to let the traditional British puddings they loved and craved become extinct'. An eccentric lot, they had an evening of sampling several puddings, all of which

FROZEN PUDDINGS

One type of dessert that had been safe from the middle and working classes was ices, or ice creams and sorbets, as we would call them now. They had been part of the realm of the super-rich since the seventeenth century, but in the Regency era, iced puddings were devised by French chefs, who thought that the beloved British pudding needed jazzing up, and leading the way was Antonin Carême. The first was Nesselrode pudding, a chestnut ice cream flavoured with rum, set in a pudding mould, and sometimes served with an ice-cold custard sauce. It really caught on and a whole plethora were created, and they became the must-have for your dessert table, assuming you could afford the equipment, the imported ice and the icehouse in which to store it.

The person responsible for making iced puddings an achievable luxury for the middle classes was Agnes B. Marshall, entrepreneur, teacher and cookery writer. She wrote two beautiful books on ices (*Book of Ices* in 1885, and *Fancy Ices* in 1894), and inside the pages of her books, you

BY ROYAL LETTERS PATENT.
MARSHALL'S PATENT FREEZER.
HIGHEST AWARD: INTERNATIONAL INVENTIONS EXHIBITION.

COMPLETE VIEW.
IS PRAISED BY ALL WHO KNOW IT
FOR
CHEAPNESS in first cost.   CLEANLINESS in working.
ECONOMY in use.   SIMPLICITY in construction.
RAPIDITY in Freezing.
No Packing necessary.   No Spatula necessary.
Smooth and Delicious Ice produced in three minutes.
SIZES—No. 1, to freeze any quantity up to 1 quart, £1. 5s.; No. 2, for 2 quarts, £1. 15s.; No. 3, for 4 quarts, £3; No. 4, for 6 quarts, £4. Reputed measure only.   Larger sizes to order.

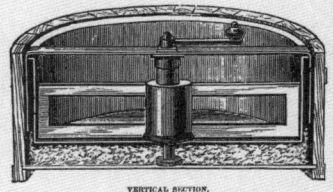

VERTICAL SECTION.
Showing the fan inside, which remains still while the pan revolves and scrapes up the film of ice as it forms on the bottom of the pan.
The ice and salt is also shown *under* the pan; there is no need to pack any round the sides.

see many wonderful illustrations of her creations, but also pages and pages of advertisements for specialist ingredients, such as gelatine and food colouring; equipment, like ice cream churns and ice boxes; and many, many moulds, all of which were Marshall-brand products.

MOULDS FOR THESE DESIGNS CAN BE HAD OF A.B. MARSHALL.

were brought into the dining room in the Parade of the Seven Puddings and introduced by the Pudding Master.[2] It is described by food historian Mary Wallace Kelsey as 'an orgy of puddings and sauces'.[3] It is still going strong.

But just as the pudding – and traditional cooking in general – was most threatened in the 1990s, British cooks came back to the fore to sing the wonders of our almost-forgotten cuisines – the likes of chefs Gary Rhodes, Rick Stein and *Two Fat Ladies*' Jennifer Paterson and Clarissa Dickson Wright. It had been a narrow squeak, but traditional foods were being coveted both in the home and on the fancy London restaurant scene. British food was back, and pudding – specifically sticky toffee pudding – led the way.

If you ask someone to rank their favourite puddings, the chances are that sticky toffee pudding will be top three, and probably number one. When I ask folk how old it is, they usually guess that it's a Victorian creation, but it is, in fact, a relative newcomer. Try googling the term 'sticky toffee pudding' and you will find no references to it before the 1970s. The earliest mention I can find is in a 1976 *Guardian* article about the chef and owner of the Sharrow Bay Hotel in Ullswater in the Lake District, Francis Coulson, the supposed inventor of the dish. He says that he came up with it in the 1960s, though rumour has it that he got it from a Lancastrian or Canadian cook. Everyone who ate it loved it, but it remained a Lake District speciality. But then came

A MERE TRIFLE

The word trifle comes from the Old French word *trufe* and means something of no, or little, importance. The first recipe can be found in Thomas Dawson's *The Good Housewife's Jewel* of 1596, a simple mixture of cream, sugar, rosewater and ground ginger. It is gently warmed so that the sugar can dissolve and the cream can thicken, then it is poured into a serving bowl. Very easy. Georgian trifles became a little more complex: macaroons were soaked in sweet wine and topped with a frothy syllabub. In the Victorian era, the custard and jam layers were added, and the classic trifle was born.

After two rounds of rationing from two world wars, coupled with our ever-increasing reliance on preparatory packet food, we really began to lose our way; trifles were now commonly made with cheap synthetically flavoured jelly, stale teacakes, harsh sherry and mock cream. For bona fide trifle-loves, the final nail in the coffin was Bird's trifle, where every element, including the 'cream', came dried in a sachet. What a relief it

Trifle.

must have been, then, when the winning pudding chosen to represent Queen Elizabeth II's Platinum Jubilee celebrations in 2022 was a trifle, complete with Swiss roll and jelly. For me, however, the joy of this competition wasn't the rehabilitation of a derided dessert, it was that it was a competition to invent *a pudding* to mark the historic occasion, an institution deemed as British as the long-reigning monarch herself.

the resurgence in interest in traditional British foods and cooking methods in the 1990s. Sticky toffee was elevated to poster child for this movement and put on a pedestal, and it was in this decade that the first recipes for it began to appear in cookery books. Now there are scores of them; every chef and food writer worth their salt has a take on the recipe. Despite it being less than 30 years old in the 1990s, it was deemed a classic, traditional British pudding, baked since time immemorial. It just goes to show how the foods we decide are traditional don't have to be old, or even from the British Isles for that matter: a pudding is traditional when we say it is.

TWENTY-FIRST-CENTURY PUDDINGS

The popularity and interest in traditional British cooking dissipated quickly in the new millennium: a time to look to the future, not to the past. In the 2010s the number of traditional puddings enjoyed at home dwindled further. Families were spending fewer and fewer hours around the dining table, and ever-busier parents found it increasingly difficult to find time to put together homemade foods of any kind, never mind puddings. The shop-bought Christmas pudding was the only time most would get a taste of a traditional boiled or steamed pud. There had never been a lower ebb, and some feared that the Christmas pudding might even go extinct. But then came the lockdowns of the Covid-19 pandemic, from March 2020, a time of great distress and uncertainty. Suddenly people turned to puddings, the ultimate comfort food, and they have remained popular ever since. Supermarkets reported a spike in sales: rice pudding sales up 45 per cent, Yorkshire pudding 80 per cent, the retro iced pudding Viennetta 20 per cent. In 2022 a million more people bought a

Christmas pudding compared to the previous year. Taken as a whole group, supermarket sales for puddings have increased by 20 per cent compared to pre-Covid times.

The pandemic forced us to take stock, and traditional puddings, it seems, had remained in our collective consciousness the entire time. This is good news, but these puddings were being bought, not made at home. While banana bread and sourdough were doing the rounds on Instagram, where were the puddings? I am putting it down to a perceived lack of skills or kit. And then, no sooner had we picked ourselves up and dusted ourselves down, we were engulfed by the cost-of-living crisis, with unpredictable and fluctuating energy prices, so it's not a surprise that we assumed that the only way we could enjoy a pudding was to outsource the cooking and buy one at the supermarket. But I believe that making puds at home *can* be good economics, and that's down to the adaptability of the pudding – it's the reason it has survived through the centuries. The trouble is, it is we who have to do the adapting: countless puddings can be made quickly (so-called hasty puddings have been around for centuries), and many can be baked alongside the roast potatoes or the lasagne on a Sunday. My brother cooks his Sussex pond pudding atop his wood-burning stove. Steamers stack, so puddings could cook along with your veg. Steamer ovens are *en vogue*, and spacious enough to steam a few puds at once, storing the remainder for later. Slow cookers make excellent rice pudding, a pressure cooker substantially reduces steam time, and you'll be amazed as to how good a microwaved sponge pudding can be – steaming is one of the handful of things microwaves do well. There are ways and there are means.

WORLD OF PUDDINGS

I have banged on throughout this book about how the pudding is a uniquely British institution, but armed with our modern, broad definition of what a pudding is, we can look around the world and find foods that, if they were made in the UK, would certainly be considered pudding. In the USA there is the banana pudding, a creamy yellow squit in a bowl made from a packet, the UK equivalent perhaps of Angel Delight. Aside from that there are no other puddings, not in name anyway, but if you leaf through *American Cookery* by Amelia Simmons, published in 1796, you will see several, including plum pudding, bread pudding and Sunderland pudding. Sadly, they are cooked no longer. But there are puddings – proper puddings – still being made and eaten: a Dutch baby is essentially a sweet Yorkshire pudding, and a baked Alaska, with its meringue, sponge cake and ice cream, is definitely a pudding. Then – and this may surprise you – there are the fruit crumbles, cobblers, slumps and grunts, all of which are already considered proper puddings in the UK but actually originated in the US. A French *clafoutis* is basically a Kentish cherry batter pudding under a different name, and *île flottante* – a poached meringue sitting in *crème anglaise* – is without a doubt a pudding. The same goes for German *Dampfnudal*, a poached dumpling sat in a sweet custardy sauce. There are Italian *tiramisu, panna cotta* and *zabaglione*; Ukrainian *syrnyky*, a curd cheesecake similar to those still baked in Yorkshire; Thai *khao niew ma muang*, coconut sticky rice with mango; and Brazilian *rabanada*, a sort of *pain perdu* made with condensed milk and eggs and seasoned with cinnamon. They are puddings all.

Then, if you travel temporally as well as spatially and take a look back in time at our food traditions, there are many recipes that, although they were not considered puddings at the time, would be welcomed into the fold today: Victorian pancakes, Georgian possets, Tudor junkets. There is a recipe in medieval cookery book *The Forme of Cury* for a delicious almond and rose pudding;

and in the fourth-century Roman text *Apicius*, there is a lovely semolina pudding. Someone somewhere and at every point of history has been eating pudding. Whether they knew it or not is a different matter.

THE FUTURE OF PUDDING

What does the future of the pudding look like? In a 2023 interview on BBC Radio 4's *The Food Programme*, food historian Ivan Day said, 'I think the future of the pudding is going to be absolutely extraordinary because of the talent that's around at the moment.'[4] I think he is correct; several fine-dining chefs have brought back that 'plain and simple' approach to British cooking. They are cooking food that comforts, food that's good for the soul. Fine dining doesn't have to be all foams, emulsions and *sous vide*, and chefs such as Fergus Henderson, Justin Gellatly and Jeremy Lee have put proper puddings back on the menu. A new pride has emerged.

At home, television programmes like *The Great British Bake Off* have helped us reconnect with our traditional bakes, and several puddings have featured on the show. Food writers and TV cooks include a good number of pudding recipes in their works: Nigella Lawson's self-saucing chocolate pudding was a revelation, and proof that a good pudding is simple to make and doesn't require any arcane equipment to pull off successfully. One person who has done much to help us return to puddings, to rekindle our love for them, is Regula Ysewijn, who took us on a wonderful tour of centuries of excellent puddings in her 2015 book *Pride and Pudding*, showing us not just the great variety of puds out there, but what we would gain by cooking them again: soothing, simple, nurturing food.

I conclude our story bursting with pride: puddings are in the ascendant once more, and you no longer have to be some kind of eccentric to be an ardent pudding-fancier (though it probably helps). What was reckoned to be the end for the British pudding turned out to be a new beginning for what is the best of all foods.

All things hes an end, and a pudding hes twa.
Scots proverb

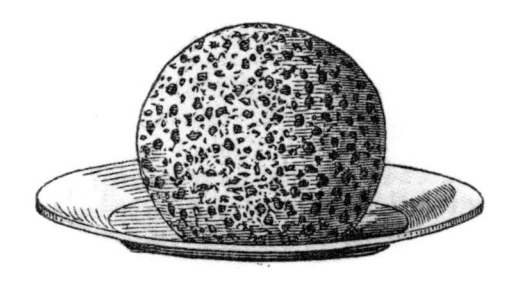

FURTHER READING AND SELECTED REFERENCES

PRIMARY SOURCES
Eliza Acton, *Modern Cookery for Private Families* (1845)
Isabella Beeton, *The Book of Household Management* (1861)
Thomas Dawson, *The Good Housewife's Jewel* (1596)
Kenelm Digby, *The Closet of the Eminently Learned Sir Kenelme Digbie Knight Opened* (1669)
Hannah Glasse, *The Art of Cookery Made Plain and Easy* (1747)
Elizabeth Raffald, *The Experienced English Housekeeper* (1769)

SECONDARY SOURCES
Peter Brears, *Cooking & Dining in the Victorian Country House* (2023)
Jan Davison, *English Sausages* (2015)
Mark Dawson, Laura Mason and Janet Pickering (eds), *Moulded Foods* (1921)
Jane Grigson, *English Food* (Third Edition, 1992)

Dorothy Hartley, *Food in England* (1954); *Lost Country Life* (1979)

F. Marian McNeill, *The Scots Kitchen: Its Lore and Recipes* (Second Edition, 1968)

Regula Ysewijn, *Pride and Pudding: The History of British Puddings Savoury and Sweet* (2015)

BLOGS AND WEBSITES

Neil Buttery, *British Food: A History*: britishfoodhistory.com

Ivan Day, *Food History Jottings*: foodhistorjottings.blogspot.com

Glyn Hughes, *The Foods of England Project*: foodsofengland.co.uk

LIST OF ILLUSTRATIONS

All images from the collections of the British Library unless otherwise credited.

p.ii © Josephine Sumner.

p.vi Plate from *Beeton's Book of Household Management*, 1879–80.

p.3 *Les Gourmands*. Anonymous print, British, late eighteenth century. (Metropolitan Museum of Art, New York)

p.6 Killing and bleeding a pig. Calendar page for December, from a book of hours (commonly known as the *Golf Book*), c.1520–30.

p.12–13 *The Accomplisht Cook* by Robert May, 1685.

p.17 Bringing in the haggis at the Royal Scottish Corporation Festival, from *The Sphere*, 7 December 1901. (Look and Learn/Bridgeman Images)

p.21 Plan for a grand table from *The Experienced English Housekeeper* by Elizabeth Raffald, 1769. (The University of Manchester Library) p.22 An advert for the Eagle Range from *Mrs A. B. Marshall's Larger Cookery Book of Extra Recipes*, 1891. (Wellcome Collection)

p.25 Advert for tin moulds from *Mrs A. B. Marshall's Larger Cookery Book of Extra Recipes*, 1891. (Wellcome Collection)

p.26 Advert for Cowan's Baking Powder from *Fancy Ices* by Mrs A. B. Marshall, 1894. (Wellcome Collection)

p.30–1 Plate from *Beeton's Everyday Cookery and Housekeeping Book*, 1888.

p.37 'Charlotte russe', from *The Royal Cookery Book* by Jules Gouffé, 1869. (Library of Congress, Washington, D.C.)

p.42 *The Recipe Book of "Atora" Refined Beef Suet*, undated [*c*.1920s].

p.49 'The Family Plum Pudding', etching by R. Seymour, London, 1830–9. (Wellcome Collection)

p.50 'Modern Mode of Serving Dishes', from *Beeton's Book of Household Management*, 1859–61.

p.53 Advert for Rizine Co.'s Fruit Jelly Flakes, *c*.1890–9. (Wellcome Collection)

p.54–5 Advert for Freeman's Pudding Powder, 1884.

p.58–9 *The Plumb-pudding in danger – or – State Epicures taking un Petit Souper* by James Gillray, 1818 (original hand-coloured cartoon first published in 1805).

p.61 Mrs Cratchit bringing in the pudding, from an illuminated manuscript of *A Christmas Carol*. (The University of Manchester Library) p.63 'Members of the United Cooks' Society preparing a monster plum pudding at Marylebone Workhouse for the Lancashire Operatives', published in the *Illustrated London News*, 3 January 1863. (Wellcome Collection)

p.64 Empire Marketing Board advert for an Empire Xmas Pudding, 1926.

p.66 The rats trying to turn Tom Kitten into a roly-poly pudding, from *The Tale of Samuel Whiskers or the Roly-Poly Pudding* by Beatrix Potter, 1908.

p.71 'Delights for the Old and Young', from *The Ideal Cook Book* by Annie R. Gregory, 1902. (Library of Congress, Washington, D.C.)

p.74 'Sultana Pudding', from *Beeton's Book of Household Management*, 1879–80.

p.80–1 'Supper Table', from *Mrs Beeton's Family Cookery and Housekeeping Book*, 1893.

p.84 Bird's Custard and puddings advert, 1920.

p.87 Advert for Marshall's Patent Freezer, from *Fancy Ices* by Mrs A. B. Marshall, 1894. (Wellcome Collection)

p.88 Advert for ice-cream moulds, from *Fancy Ices* by Mrs A. B. Marshall, 1894. (Wellcome Collection)

p.91 'Trifle', from *Beeton's Book of Household Management*, 1892.

p.96 'Royal Pudding', from *Fancy Ices* by Mrs A. B. Marshall, 1894. (Wellcome Collection)

p.98 'Boiled Pudding', from *Modern Cookery for Private Families* by Eliza Acton, 1865.

p.104 Advert for Bird's Custard, 1939.

GINGER PUDDING
WITH
BIRD'S CUSTARD HOT
... there's nothing like
BIRD'S
CUSTARD & JELLIES

ENDNOTES

1 Taken from 'Yorkshire Arms, Toasts and Sayings' series (1907) by Jack Broadrick
2 Kelsey, M. W. (1995), 'The Pudding Club and Traditional British Puddings', in H. Walker (ed.) *Disappearing Foods: Studies in Foods and Dishes at Risk: Proceedings of the Oxford Symposium on Food and Cookery 1994*, Prospect Books, p.6
3 Kelsey (1995), p.117
4 'A Pudding Celebration' (2023), *The Food Programme*, BBC Sounds

Also available in this series

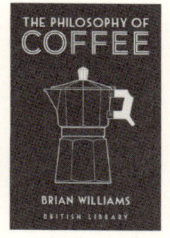

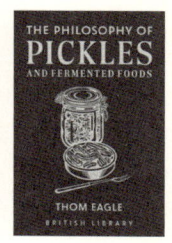

- THE PHILOSOPHY OF WHISKY — BILLY ABBOTT
- THE PHILOSOPHY OF WINE — RUTH BALL
- THE PHILOSOPHY OF CURRY — SEJAL SUKHADWALA
- THE PHILOSOPHY OF TEA — TONY GEBELY
- THE PHILOSOPHY OF GIN — JANE PEYTON
- THE PHILOSOPHY OF CHEESE — PATRICK McGUIGAN
- THE PHILOSOPHY OF BEER — JANE PEYTON
- THE PHILOSOPHY OF TATTOOS — JOHN MILLER
- THE PHILOSOPHY OF COFFEE — BRIAN WILLIAMS
- THE PHILOSOPHY OF COCKTAILS — JANE PEYTON
- THE PHILOSOPHY OF CHOCOLATE — SAM BILTON
- THE PHILOSOPHY OF CIDER — JANE PEYTON
- THE PHILOSOPHY OF PICKLES AND FERMENTED FOODS — THOM EAGLE